TO YOUR NAME

A Study of the Psalms

Volume 2

by Hal Hammons

2016 One Stone Press.
All rights reserved. No part of this book may be reproduced
in any form without written permission of the publisher.

Published by:
One Stone Press
979 Lovers Lane
Bowling Green, KY 42103

Printed in the United States of America

ISBN (10 Digit): 1-941422-18-7
ISBN (13 Digit): 978-1-941422-18-2

Unless otherwise noted, all Scripture quotations are taken from the Holman Christian Standard Bible®, Copyright © 1999, 2000, 2002, 2003 by Holman Bible Publishers. Used by Permission. Holman Christian Standard Bible®, Holman CSB®, and HCSB® are federally registered trademarks of Holman Bible Publishers.

Supplemental Materials Available:
PowerPoint slides for each lesson
Answer key
Downloadable PDF

Table of Contents

Psalm 29—A Song for the Worshiper 11
Figure of Speech: The Voice of the LORD
A Bible Study: Solomon
A Parallel Study: Psalm 100
A Case Study: Symone
New Testament Insight: Psalm 29:8
A Hymn Study: "Holy, Holy, Holy"
A Worship Study

Psalm 32—A Song for the Forgiven 21
Figure of Speech: Bit and Bridle
A Bible Study: Manasseh
A Parallel Study: Psalm 103
A Case Study: Marshall
New Testament Insight: Psalm 103:15-16
A Hymn Study: "I Will Sing of My Redeemer"
A Worship Study

Psalm 40—A Song for the Patient 31
Figure of Speech: The Hairs of My Head
A Bible Study—Abraham
A Parallel Study: Psalm 25
A Case Study: Alan and Sue
New Testament Insight: Psalm 25:3
A Hymn Study: "Have Thine Own Way Lord"
A Worship Study

Psalm 42—A Song for the Depressed 41
Figure of Speech: Deep Calls to Deep
A Bible Study: Naomi
A Parallel Study: Psalm 22
A Case Study: Jeffrey
New Testament Insight: Psalm 22:1
A Hymn Study: "Be Still, My Soul"
A Worship Study

Psalm 46—A Song for the Fearful 53
Figure of Speech: He Makes Wars Cease
A Bible Study: King Asa
A Parallel Study: Psalm 56
A Case Study: Arthur
New Testament Insight: Psalm 46:4
A Hymn Study: "Eternal Father, Strong To Save"
A Worship Study

Psalm 49—A Song for the Wealthy 63
Figure of Speech: Sheol
A Bible Study: Church in Laodicea
A Parallel Study: Psalm 73
A Case Study: Liam
New Testament Insight: Psalm 49:7-9
A Hymn Study: "Be With Me, Lord"
A Worship Study

Psalm 50—A Song for the Hypocrite 73
Figure of speech: A Thousand Hills
A Bible Study: Woman Caught in Adultery
A Parallel Study: Psalm 15
A Case Study: Paula
New Testament Insight: Psalm 50:11
A Hymn Study: "Deeper and Deeper"
A Worship Study

Psalm 51—A Song for the Guilty 83
Figure of Speech: Guilty When I Was Born
A Bible Study: David
A Parallel Study: Psalm 38
A Case Study: Dean
New Testament Insight: Psalm 51:2
A Hymn Study: "Cleanse Me"
A Worship Study

Psalm 52—A Song for the Enemy 93
Figure of speech: A Sharpened Razor
A Bible Study: Ahab
A Parallel Study: Psalm 94
A Case Study: Avery
New Testament Insight: Psalm 94:13-14
A Hymn Study: "The Battle Hymn of the Republic"
A Worship Study

Psalm 59—A Song for the Persecuted 105
Figure of speech: Dogs
A Bible Study: Jeremiah
A Parallel Study: Psalm 69
A Case Study: Jill
New Testament Insight: Psalm 69:8-9
A Hymn Study: "We Gather Together"
A Worship Study

Psalm 75—A Song for the Thankful.. 115
Figure of speech: Lift Up Your Horn
A Bible Study: Jews and Samaritans
A Parallel Study: Psalm 136
A Case Study: Leana
New Testament Insight: Psalm 136:21-22
A Hymn Study: "Count Your Blessings"
A Worship Study

Psalm 91—A Song for Life 127
Figure of speech: God's Wings
A Bible Study: Ezekiel's Vision of the Valley of Dry Bones
A Parallel Study: Psalm 139
A Case Study: Elise
New Testament Insight: Psalm 91:11
A Hymn Study: "In Heavenly Love Abiding"
A Worship Study

To Your Name
An Introduction for the Reader

On Friday, November 13, 2015, terrorists attacked Paris, France. Six venues, including a soccer stadium holding tens of thousands of people, were struck. More than 150 were killed.

Three days later on live television, *The Voice* contestant Jordan Smith performed "Great is Thy Faithfulness," a hymn written almost a century before by Thomas Chisholm ("Be With Me," "Bring Christ Your Broken Life," "Only in Thee," etc.) Within an hour the song had risen to #2 on the iTunes pop chart. Clearly, people felt the need to have someone remind them of the faithful God—always watching, always loving, sometimes invisible but always present. *Strength for today and bright hope for tomorrow, Blessings all mine, with ten thousand beside!*

Words have power. Words accompanied by music, even more so.

My love for spiritual singing feeds my love for the Psalms. Whether the words are tweaked slightly and set to music, or whether the sentiments are adopted and rephrased, or whether I am simply reading the text as it is and imagining the host of Israel singing a melody unheard, it is perhaps worship in its purest form. That, in a rather large nutshell, is the reason for *To Your Name*.

You may ask, "Why two volumes?" At the risk of sounding simplistic, one was too few and three were too many. The two parts of this series cover 24 of the psalms in some detail, and reserve significant time for the consideration of 24 more. That is almost a third of them—enough to give the reader a fairly good overview of the longest book in the Bible. (I would venture to suggest two quarters of material in Job, Isaiah or Ezekiel would leave a lot of meat on the bone as well.) But the Psalter is, by its nature, somewhat repetitive. Extending the format of these two books to include a third would be forced. So, two. And if your favorite or the one that puzzles you the most is still left out, I apologize.

For those who may be starting with Volume 2, for whatever reason, a recap of how the book works:
- Each lesson will feature a single psalm, focusing on a particular audience and a particular message. The lesson will help you study the psalm in question in seven different ways:
- A brief look at the psalm itself.
- An insight into the use of figurative language as it is used in the psalm.
- A Bible lesson about a character who fits in the scope of the psalm.
- A secondary psalm to study in brief, helping to show the pattern of topic development throughout the Psalter.
- A "case study" of a person in the modern day that relates to the topic at hand.
- A look into the New Testament at a story, character or text that is brought into sharper relief by considering a verse or term from one of the two selected psalms.

- Finally, a modern-day hymn relating to the topic, and a discussion of how we can use hymns of this nature to emphasize points being taught in the psalm.

This is a lot of studying to do. It was written with the idea that a group could spend two 45-minute sessions on each lesson. The teacher notes included here will follow that plan. However, individual teachers and classes are encouraged to proceed at their own pace, whether faster or slower.

As of this writing, I still haven't started the study to which I allude in the "A Worship Study" section. Dare to dream, Hal. The people referenced therein, as well as the case studies, are also fictitious. Similarities to actual persons are not intended and should not be inferred.

Again, thanks to Tim Berman for typesetting the hymns. Thanks to Andy Alexander, Steve Curtis and the crew at One Stone for everything they do to get everything between two covers and on shelves. Thanks to the brethren and elders at East Hill for their constant encouragement and patience. Thanks to hymn writers and composers everywhere. And if you have read the first volume of *To Your Name* and seen fit to read this one as well, thanks to you.

Finally, my brethren:
>*Not to us LORD, not to us,*
>*but to Your name give glory*
>*because of Your faithful love, because of Your truth. (Psalm 115:1)*

Hal Hammons
Pace, Florida
December 2015

Teachers Notes

The following is a suggested plan for a class schedule using *To Your Name*, assuming two 45-minute class periods per lesson:

Class 1:

- Read the primary psalm aloud from the book. (5 minutes)
- Discuss the psalm and answer the questions. (20 minutes)
- Discuss figures of speech, including the one highlighted. (5 minutes)
- Discuss the "Bible Study" section and answer the questions. (15 minutes)
- Read the primary psalm aloud again if time permits.

Class 2:

- Discuss the secondary psalm; read it aloud from the text of the reader's choosing if it is not too long. (15 minutes)
- Discuss the "Case Study" section, and answer the questions. (10 minutes)
- Discuss the "New Testament Insight" section. (10 minutes)
- Discuss the "Hymn Study" and "Worship Study" sections, and discuss students' answers to the "Worship Study" question. Sing the song as a group if you wish. (10 minutes)
- If time permits, discuss other appropriate or inappropriate hymns along the same theme.

To Matt Bassford, Craig Roberts, Tim Stevens,
and everyone else who loves song worship enough
to teach others how to do it properly.

Psalm 29
A Song for the Worshiper

Why should we worship our God? The "heavenly beings" called to worship in Psalm 29 should be righteous enough so as to not need reminding. In reminding ourselves, it emphasizes to us again (as is necessary on a frequent basis) what we are actually doing when we come before our Creator.

David emphasizes worshiping God because of His nature. It is His due. Although we cannot literally give God any more glory and strength (or any other attribute) than He already has, we can magnify Him by making Him great in the eyes of those who do not yet acknowledge Him. The emphasis in the first two verses on the greatness of God supports the insertion of the word "His" with reference to the holiness involved in worship. Although we must make ourselves holy in His presence, His own holiness is the subject of discussion here.

Verses 3-9 describe His power. By simply speaking, He accomplishes things far beyond the greatest human endeavors. His reach extends "above vast waters;" the storms we see miles offshore are as much His handiwork as those we experience firsthand. The same goes for activity in foreign lands. He speaks His will far to the north, to Lebanon and the snowy peaks of Mount Hermon—called Sirion here and in Deuteronomy 3:8-9. He reaches southward to Kadesh, where Israel was condemned to death in the wilderness by the wrath of the God for refusing to enter Canaan (Numbers 13-14). His

¹ Give the LORD—you heavenly beings—
give the LORD glory and strength.
² Give the LORD the glory due His name;
worship the LORD in the splendor of His holiness.
³ The voice of the LORD is above the waters.
The God of glory thunders—
the LORD, above vast waters,
⁴ the voice of the LORD in power,
the voice of the LORD in splendor.
⁵ The voice of the LORD breaks the cedars;
the LORD shakes the cedars of Lebanon.
⁶ He makes Lebanon skip like a calf,
and Sirion, like a young wild ox.
⁷ the voice of the LORD flashes flames of fire.
⁸ The voice of the LORD shakes the wilderness;
the LORD shakes the wilderness of Kadesh.
⁹ The voice of the LORD makes the deer give birth
and strips the woodlands bare.
In His temple all cry, "Glory!"
¹⁰ The LORD sat enthroned at the flood,
the LORD sits enthroned, King forever.
¹¹ The LORD gives His people strength; the LORD blesses His people with peace.

power is so impressive and undeniable, it is said to cause premature birth in animals and uproot entire forests.

Verses 10-11 speak to His authority. The creation stands as it does because the flood formed it so, just as He formed the pre-flood world in the beginning. And His destruction and regeneration are every bit as much a testimony of His reign as King as the original six days of Genesis 1 are. Thankfully, we have willingly submitted to His rule, and as such receive strength and peace from His hand instead of wrath and punishment. Who would not want to worship such a God? Who would dare not worship?

1. Read verse 2 in multiple versions. List some other ways the term "splendor of His holiness" is translated. Which do you think fits the context the best?
   _____
   _____
   _____
   _____

2. The New American Standard Bible renders the phrase, "Worship the LORD in holy array." Does this or any other passage stress the importance of the clothing we are to wear as we worship? _____
   _____
   _____
   _____
   _____

3. Over what is God "King forever?" What implications does that have for worship? _____
   _____
   _____
   _____

4. What is your favorite line in the psalm and why? _____
   _____
   _____
   _____

The Worshiper: A Bible Study

It was like no worship service any of them had ever seen. It was like no worship service that had ever been conducted, anywhere, by anyone, at any time. In terms of participation, scope, historical significance, and sheer spectacle, surely it must have been the greatest worship service that has ever been—or that ever will be on this side of eternity.

Solomon had been preparing to build a temple to his God. His father, David, had put elements in place perhaps even before Solomon was born. Now, finally, all was ready. The temple was finished. New artifacts had been fashioned. Participants had been trained. Most of all, the ark of the covenant had been placed

> **Figure of Speech**
>
> **The Voice of the LORD**
>
> A few passages record an actual sound being associated with God—most notably, perhaps, at Mount Sinai (Exodus 20:18-19) and on a small number of occasions during Jesus' ministry (Matthew 3:17, 17:5; John 12:28). The events at Sinai especially indicate the awe and fear inspired in the heart of the one who finds himself in the presence of the Creator of all. Although we should not believe God just speaks because He likes breaking trees in half, there is definitely something to be said for remembering that His voice has that power, whether we see Him using it or not.
>
> Hebrews 1:1 reads, "Long ago God spoke to the fathers by the prophets at different times and in different ways." Notice, though, it was God who spoke. The agency of a prophet did not detract from the original Source of the message. Regardless of whether the "voice" comes directly from heaven, through the mouth or pen of a prophet, or through us as we read, it is God who is speaking.

in a permanent home for the first time in its history. It was a time for celebration. And celebrate they did. However, it was not merely a day for celebrating national success or even Solomon's own success; it was a day for celebrating the presence of the Lord God.

In many ways, the opening of the temple was much like one of our worship services today, writ large. There was prayer (2 Chronicles 6:12-42). There was music as authorized by God in the Law of Moses (2 Chronicles 5:11-13). Solomon himself delivered a stirring message (2 Chronicles 6:1-11). The contributions made to the work of the temple were astounding (2 Chronicles 7:4-7).

Communion was the most important element. The temple was to be God's house; having the temple in the land reassured the people that they were in the presence of God, and coming to honor Him in that temple was both a duty and a privilege. God showed Solomon and the nation His acceptance of their offering by giving the appearance of literally taking up residence in His house: "the LORD's temple, was filled with a cloud. And because of the cloud, the priests were not able to continue ministering, for the glory of the LORD filled God's temple" (2 Chronicles 5:13-14).

Read Psalm 29 again—this time with Solomon in mind.

1. Was such an elaborate display necessary to consecrate a temple for a God who cannot possibly be housed in a physical location (Isaiah 66:1-2)? _____
_____
_____

2. Find another example of the presence of God being demonstrated in a cloud.

Psalm 100—A Parallel Study

If a person appears disengaged (or even downright hostile) during the song portion of our worship, in which one's attitude naturally shows more easily, is it safe to assume their attitude is the same during a study of God's word? Or communion? Or prayer? What impact does their attitude have on the attitude of the body as a whole? Surely not a positive one.

This is one reason among many why it is important to "shout triumphantly to the LORD" (v.1), to "come before Him with joyful songs" (v.2). If we cannot manage any enthusiasm while we are singing about the greatness of our God and the depth of His blessings, we will give people the impression we are not emotionally engaged. This impression may be correct.

People emote in different ways and to different degrees. If one genuinely cannot find joy in worshiping, it is time for them to consider the possibility that God is just not a big part of their life—and to consider the implications.

1. What things in this life make you smile? Why? Should God be as much or more of a source of happiness as carnal things?

2. What are the implications for worship in verse 3—"Acknowledge that the LORD is God, He made us, and we are His?"

3. What does God's "faithfulness" (v.5) imply? How should we show faithfulness to Him?

4. What is your favorite line in the psalm and why?

The Worshiper: A Case Study

"We have a problem in our song service," Jason said with his wife, Margot, to one of the elders after worship services one Sunday. "And frankly, it is becoming impossible for us to sing in a worshipful mind."

"It's Symone," Margot followed. "And we love Symone. Who couldn't? But she sings so loudly, and so off-key, we just can't keep our mind on the Lord."

"Well, that's a problem," the elder said.

"And we know that there are more important things than the quality of the sound in our singing," Margot said. "But we just had a lesson last month about doing whatever we do for the Lord to the best of our ability. Doesn't that include singing?"

"Of course," the elder said, nodding.

"We thought it was adorable the first few months they were worshiping with us," Jason said. "But it's not adorable anymore. We expect our children to behave themselves at church services, to not be a distraction to anyone. That's our job. And we think it's reasonable to expect other parents to do the same."

"Obviously, we feel a bit funny complaining about a child's behavior, us being adults," Margot said. "But John and Rachel are adults, too. It's not fair of them to let their child go unrestrained and have the rest of us just try to deal with it somehow."

"You could move, I suppose."

"I don't think that would help," Jason said. "We were distracted by her when they were sitting on the other side of the auditorium last year. I mean, don't you hear her?" The elder nodded. "Right. And you usually sit back where they used to be. So you know what we're talking about. Besides, not to be petty, but we were there first."

"Have you talked to John and Rachel about it?"

"We've wanted to, dozens of times. But how do you tell a child's parents that she needs to be less enthusiastic in church? I mean, plenty of children don't participate in church services at all."

"That's right," the elder said. "So basically you want me to do your dirty work for you."

"No, no, it's not like that," Margot hastened to say.

"It's OK, I'm an elder. It comes with the territory. In fact, I'll do it now." Catching the eye of John, who was carrying Symone on his way out the door, he motioned for him to walk over and join them. Embarrassed, Margot quickly walked away as John approached.

The elder poked Symone in the ribs playfully. "It has come to my attention that you have been voted the most enthusiastic singer in the whole church. What do you have to say about that, young lady?" Grinning, Symone buried her face in John's shoulder. "Well I just wanted to tell you and your daddy that you got my vote, too, and that we are very, *very* proud of you. Proud of you all." He shook John's free hand and patted him on the shoulder, and tousled Symone's hair a bit. John walked away beaming.

"All right then," the elder said, turning back to Jason. "Was there anything else you wanted to talk about?"

Read Psalm 29 again—this time, with Symone in mind.

What would you say to Symone and her family based on Psalm 29? _____
_____
_____
_____

New Testament Insight

The voice of the LORD shakes the wilderness;
the LORD shakes the wilderness of Kadesh. — *Psalm 29:8*

The critics of Jesus continually asked Him for "a sign from heaven" (Matthew 16:1)—that is, a demonstration of power outside the behavior of himself and others. Joel prophesied that such behavior would characterize the gospel age—that in addition to prophecies and other outpourings of the Spirit, He would "display wonders in the heavens and on the earth" (Joel 2:29-30). Apparently, healing the blind and raising the dead was not enough proof for them; they needed to hear from God Himself.

Well, they did hear. Admittedly, the audience for the divine voice at Jesus' baptism—"You are My beloved Son; I take delight in You" (Mark 1:11)—was limited; at the transfiguration (Mark 9:7) even more so. A large crowd, not just of close disciples, heard the voice in the temple courtyard promising to further glorify Jesus' name (John 12:28). Jesus' frequent admonition, "Anyone who has ears to hear should listen!" (Luke 8:8), would seem to apply perfectly here. If they would not listen to the voice of God, He would "speak" in even more remarkable ways in the days that followed. Matthew 27:50-53 tells of the torn temple curtain, an earthquake, and even the dead released from their tombs. And the greatest message of all would follow shortly—the empty tomb (Mark 16:6).

The Worshiper: A Hymn Study

Reginald Heber was an Anglican clergyman in a small congregation near Birmingham, England in the early 19th Century. He was preparing a lesson for Trinity Sunday, which is the Sunday following Pentecost and celebrates the doctrine of the threefold personality of Deity—Father, Son, and Holy Spirit. He had developed an ability to write hymns to counteract what he felt was subpar singing in churches, particularly his congregation. "Holy, Holy, Holy" acknowledged and praised "God in three persons, blessed Trinity." Heber borrowed heavily from John's vision recorded in Revelation 4. After 16 years of service in his native England, Heber served as Bishop of Calcutta in India for three years. He died suddenly while traveling in Trichinopoly, India, on April 3, 1826, at the age of 42.

A collection of Heber's hymns was put together shortly after his death. The most famous today by far is "Holy, Holy, Holy," in large measure resulting from the majestic music written for it by John Bacchus Dykes, the well-known hymn composer. Dykes wrote the music in 1861 and entitled the tune "Nicaea," after the First Council of Nicaea that affirmed the doctrine of the Trinity.

Heber's lyrics have been adjusted somewhat over the years, most notably by the Unitarians. Rejecting the concept of the Trinity, the Unitarians substituted the phrase, "God over all, and blest eternally" for the original, "God in three persons, blessed Trinity." Many Christians today reject the term "Trinity" as having no basis in Scripture; therefore, many hymnals, including most of the ones produced by brethren, prefer the substitute line—penned, ironically, by those who were specifically trying to deny the deity of Jesus Christ.

The Worshiper: A Worship Study

Our best (in my mind) song worship leader was a middle-aged widower, retired early from a successful career, no real musical training, but plenty of God-given talent and a will to worship. "It's nice to sing the tenor part for a change on that one," he said after we sang "Holy, Holy, Holy."

"What do you mean?" I asked.

He paused for a moment. "I've probably sung "Holy, Holy, Holy" more than any other hymn in the book. Part of that, of course, is that it is a popular choice and has been ever since I can remember. Part of it also is because it got me through the toughest time in my life.

"When Greta died, I was devastated. Some of you remember. Not having children, she was my whole world, other than the Lord, of course. Some people say the nights are the toughest time, but it wasn't for me. I would just keep myself occupied with TV or a good book until I couldn't keep my eyes open, and then I'd fall asleep; in my recliner, as often as not.

"The worst part for me was the morning. Waking up and being alone. Knowing I would miss her for the rest of the day. For whatever reason, that was the part I could not get past. I stayed there for an entire month.

"Then, something came over me. I decided I would not spend another month wallowing. I was, and am, tremendously blessed, with or without my wife. It wasn't right for me to act otherwise. So I decided I would spend my mornings with God for the next month.

"I set my alarm to go off before sunrise. I forced myself to go to bed at a decent hour. I woke up the next morning still unclear as to what exactly I was going to do, but determined to trust God to get me through. I took my Bible out into the backyard and sat in the gazebo where Greta and I used to drink our morning coffee. Immediately I thought of the line from that hymn—"Early in the morning our song shall rise to Thee." And since I didn't have a better idea, I just sang the song softly to myself and God, all four stanzas by memory. Then I prayed. I tried to focus on giving Him thanks for my years with Greta, for the beauty of the sunrise, for everything. By that time, there was enough light to read, so I read for a half-hour or so from the Psalms. It was the most peaceful morning I had had since she passed.

"So I decided to do the same thing every morning for a month, except change things up a bit to keep it fresh. I made a point of offering different prayers every day, and I bounced around in several passages in the Bible. But for whatever reason, I kept singing the same song every day. "Holy, Holy, Holy."

"Didn't it start losing its meaning for you?" I asked.

"Nope."

What does "Holy, Holy, Holy" mean to you?
_____
_____
_____

The Bible Study Song List

If you were putting a list together for a study about worshiping, what songs would you include and why? _____
_____
_____

What songs might you exclude and why? _____
_____
_____

Psalm 32
A Song for the Forgiven

Happiness is elusive for many people—perhaps because they don't comprehend what "happiness" is. They think if they can fill their house with things, their car with family, and their days with pleasant distraction, their lives will be ideal. So they spend every waking moment in pursuit of one or more of those things, and often they succeed. Yet happiness remains elusive. It is always the next accomplishment, not the last one, holding the key to happiness.

Jesus' commentary on the "happy" or "blessed" life in the Beatitudes (Matthew 5:3-12) helps us realize the pell-mell pursuit of satisfaction in the earthly realm is ill-conceived. We find true happiness in the conquest of what keeps us from being happy in the first place. For the answer, we must go back to the Garden of Eden. Paradise was lost because of sin. The happiness God offers us—complete and utter joy—can only be found by restoring that fellowship to what it was before.

David sinned often. David had many dark days. It is no coincidence sin and dark days have a tendency to be associated with each other. David, whom God called "a man after My heart" (Acts 13:22, 1 Samuel 13:14), was genuinely grieved when he found himself drifting from his God. Perhaps we are even intended to take from verses 3-4 that David's guilt took a dramatic physical toll on his body, in addition to the emotional strain guilt brings.

¹ How happy is the one whose
   transgression is forgiven,
  whose sin is covered!
² How happy is the man the LORD
   does not charge with sin,
  and in whose spirit is no deceit!
³ When I kept silent, my bones
   became brittle
  from my groaning all day long.
⁴ For day and night Your hand
   was heavy on me;
  my strength was drained
   as in the summer's heat.
⁵ Then I acknowledged my sin to
   You
  and did not conceal my iniquity.
  I said,
  "I will confess my transgressions
   to the LORD,"
  and you took away the guilt of
   my sin.

⁶ Therefore let everyone who is
   faithful pray to You
   at a time that You may be found.
   When great floodwaters come,
   they will not reach him.
⁷ You are my hiding place;
   You protect me from trouble.
   You surround me with joyful
   shouts of deliverance.
⁸ I will instruct you and show you
   the way to go;
   with My eye on you, I will give
   counsel.
⁹ Do not be like a horse or mule,
   without understanding,
   that must be controlled with bit
   and bridle,
   or else it will not come near you.
¹⁰ Many pains come to the wicked,
   but the one who trusts in the
   LORD
   will have faithful love surrounding him.
¹¹ Be glad in the LORD and rejoice,
   you righteous ones;
   shout for joy,
   all you upright in heart.

Confessing wrongdoing is not a natural action. It requires humility. It is a tacit acceptance of our failure and inadequacy. Many people seem incapable of even the most basic of apologies. But the true child of God not only acknowledges the existence of his sin (Romans 3:23), he accepts responsibility for it and begs for forgiveness.

"Be glad in the LORD and rejoice, you righteous ones; shout for joy, all you upright in heart," David writes in the final verse of the psalm. Truly, the righteous cannot find any significant gladness anywhere else. What a shame it is that we often, like David, wait so long in miserable stubbornness and rebellion before reaching out for it.

1. What conditions are given in the New Testament for the forgiveness or "covering" of sins? _____
_____
_____
_____
_____
_____

2. How might I attempt to "conceal my iniquity?" What do such attempts really accomplish? _____
_____
_____
_____
_____
_____

3. Do wicked people suffer "many pains" (v.10) because of their refusal to confess their sins? If so, how? _____
_____
_____
_____
_____
_____

> ### Figure of Speech
> #### Bit and Bridle
>
> Although donkeys typically are used in figurative texts to connote images of stubbornness, such is not necessarily the case for horses and mules. Horses and mules are work animals that must go where their owners direct to be functional. The bit and bridle turn the animal in the proper direction—a direction it likely would not choose and in which it almost certainly would not persist if left to itself.
>
> God spoke to King Hezekiah and the nation of Judah in 2 Kings 19:27-28, saying the salvation they were about to receive from the Assyrian oppression was despite their attitude, not because of it. Since the nation had proved resistant to choosing God's path, God would practically force them to accept His way. Of course, all of us have free will. Just as the horse can fight against the bit and bridle (to its detriment), so also the people of God can (and, in the case of Judah) and do find a way to "spit the bit." Far better for us to choose His path on our own than wait for God to force us—and then resent Him for it.

4. What is your favorite line in the psalm and why? _____
_____
_____
_____

The Forgiven: A Bible Study

We are hard pressed to select the worst king in Israel's history. Manasseh ought to receive some consideration. As the son of Hezekiah, one of the greatest spiritual reformers in the history of the nation, Manasseh wasted little time in undoing all of Hezekiah's work in the cause of God. Perhaps receiving the throne at the tender age of 12 had something to do with it. In any case, 2 Chronicles 33:1-9 details the abominations Manasseh perpetrated, including actually bringing an idol into the temple of God itself. Verse 9 summarizes: "So Manasseh caused Judah and the inhabitants of Jerusalem to stray so that they did worse evil than the nations the LORD had destroyed before the Israelites."

Most of the time, God allowed sinful kings in Judah to stay in power, free to make whatever heinous choice and alliance they wished. However, He made an exception for Manasseh, bringing the king of Assyria to haul Manasseh with hooks into imprisonment in the city of Babylon. Clearly, this chastening was the best thing that could have happened to Manasseh. "When he was in distress, he sought the favor of the LORD his God and earnestly humbled himself before the God of his ancestors. He prayed to Him, so He heard his petition and granted his request, and brought him back to Jerusalem, to his kingdom. So Manasseh came to know that the LORD is God" (2 Chronicles 33:12-13).

Manasseh's repentance was not shallow and fake. The record goes on to detail real religious reform at the hand of Manasseh. He removed the temple idol and other abominations and encouraged the people to serve God and Him alone. It was undoubtedly a horrific way to learn his lesson, but better learn it the hard way than not learn it at all.

Read Psalm 32 again—this time with Manasseh in mind.

1. Briefly summarize the two generations of kings before and after Manasseh. What lesson should we draw with regard to parents and grandparents? ____
   _____
   _____
   _____

2. Why are lessons learned the hard way so often learned better and retained longer? _____
   _____
   _____
   _____

The Forgiven: A Case Study

Case File

Marshall
- 31 years old
- Married
- Coming back to the church after years away

Marshall was like any number of other young men in the church. He was regular but not motivated while at home. Then he went away to college in a distant part of the country, got distracted, became caught up in worldly matters, and became more and more comfortable with giving God less and less. He attended church services with his parents on the rare occasions he visited, but he saw it as more of a family obligation than a spiritual gesture. Oddly, he never saw himself as "unfaithful." He was still a Christian at heart, though—or so he thought.

He met Molly through mutual friends; three crazy weeks later, they found themselves in front of a judge in Hawaii getting married. When he brought her back home for Thanksgiving a few months later, he anticipated questions from his parents about her faith. (She was agnostic and indifferent.) As he explained his upbringing to Molly and how they would handle the "religion thing," it began to dawn on him how little a part God had been playing in his life. But it didn't really hit home until his father asked him to lead the prayer at dinner. Words completely failed him. He had forgotten how to pray. He abruptly excused himself, rushed back to his old bedroom, and found himself crying.

He was in the family pew that Sunday morning, along with Molly. They spent much of the next week talking to each other and his parents about the Bible and his resurging faith. Molly didn't understand it, didn't share it, and didn't like it. The next Sunday morning, Marshall came forward, confessing his failures and asking for prayers. Molly wasn't there. "It feels good," Marshall said to everyone, all his old friends who had been praying for him. All the time he was thinking to himself, "It should feel better than this." It didn't. And he knew why.

As the weeks progressed, friction grew in Marshall and Molly's marriage. "You've made this bed," Marshall's father told him during one of many conversations. "Sin has consequences, including some that come after you've tried to make things right. But Molly's a good woman, and she loves you. You just have to stay strong, keep trusting in the Lord, and building your faith. One of these days she will see what your relationship with Jesus means to you."

"But Dad," Marshall countered, tears in his eyes, "He meant nothing to me for so long. Nothing. How can I expect her to believe that He means everything to me now?"

Read Psalm 32 again—this time with Marshall in mind.

What would you say to Marshall based on Psalm 32?

_____
_____
_____

Psalm 103—A Parallel Study

"Do not forget all His benefits," Psalm 103:2 exhorts us. Then, as though to make sure we don't, we have some of them cataloged for us. And the first one mentioned, appropriately, is, "He forgives all your sin." Surely all of the others fade into insignificance without this one.

Forgiveness is the only one of the enumerated blessings upon which the psalmist elaborates. It is a sign of His compassionate and gracious nature. Like an earthly father who is provoked to wrath occasionally by children who disappoint, our heavenly Father "will not always accuse us or be angry forever (v.9). He loves us too much to do otherwise. Truly, "He has not dealt with us as our sins deserve (v.10). God does not excuse children of dust from acting earthly, but He forgives them when they put themselves in the path of God's grace.

As we continue to sin, we make no excuses for ourselves—and we try not to "continue in sin in order that grace may multiply" (Romans 6:1). However, thanks be to God, grace multiplies anyway. Its breadth extends "as far as the east is from the west" (v.12), "from eternity to eternity" (v.17). What a shame we need it, but what a blessing we have it!

1. Describe how God "satisfies with goodness" (v. 5) and how this might renew your youth. How might a Christian act who is not "satisfied?" _____
   _____
   _____
   _____

2. How would you define "those who fear Him" (v. 11)? How does it fit with the description of a loving, compassionate God? _____
   _____
   _____
   _____

3. Explain how verse 19 and the concept of God's sovereignty fit in the context of the psalm. _____
   _____
   _____
   _____

4. What is your favorite line in the psalm and why? _____
   _____
   _____
   _____

New Testament Insight

As for man, his days are like grass—
he blooms like a flower of the field;
when the wind passes over it, it vanishes,
and its place is no longer known.   — Psalm 103:15-16

The transient nature of life on earth is addressed several times in the Psalms. Psalm 39:4-5 reads, "LORD, reveal to me the end of my life and the number of my days. Let me know how transitory I am...Yes, every mortal man is only a vapor." The point here is whatever moments God gives us should be used wisely—particularly in pursuit of His things. The point in Psalm 103 is man's impact on his world is nothing in comparison to God's. Although man comes and goes with the wind, God and His love for His people is "from eternity to eternity" (v.17).

Both points are part of the message in James 4:13-14. It reads, "Come now, you who say, 'Today or tomorrow we will travel to such and such a city and spend a year there and do business and make a profit.' You don't even know what tomorrow will bring—what your life will be! For you are a bit of smoke that appears for a little while, then vanishes."

As James goes on to say, it is boastful to claim to have more control over the world around us than we do. It is God who holds the future, not us. Instead of boasting in the future which may never be, we should be finding and pursuing God's plan for our lives. As James 4:17 tells us, failing to do so, "it is a sin."

The Forgiven: A Hymn Study

Philip Bliss, one of the greatest hymn writers of the 19th Century, was killed on December 29, 1876, in what was at the time the worst railroad accident in American history. A bridge over the Ashtabula River collapsed under the train carrying him and his wife, along with 156 others. When his belongings were gathered from the wreckage, a hymn, as yet not set to music, was found in one of Bliss's bags, entitled, "I Will Sing of My Redeemer."

The loss of Bliss—at the time one of the most famous musicians in the country, regardless of genre—sent shockwaves through the religious community. Shortly after the crash, James McGranahan, a prominent hymn writer and composer in his own right, came upon the lyric. He penned the music for it known today. McGranahan, who had written the tune for "None of Self and All of Thee" in 1876, went on to compose the music for hymns such as "I Know Whom I Have Believed," "The Banner of the Cross," "Christ Returneth" and "Christ Receiveth Sinful Men."

"I Will Sing of My Redeemer" appears to have been one of the first songs ever recorded. George Stebbins, a preacher and musician who joined the D.L. Moody revival tour shortly after Bliss's death, is said to have used the song to demonstrate the invention of the phonograph by Thomas Edison.

I Will Sing of My Redeemer

Words: Philip P. Bliss
Music: James McGranahan

A♭ - 3/4 - SOL

The Forgiven: A Worship Study

"Let me ask you all something," I said after we sang "I Will Sing of My Redeemer." "What does it mean to 'redeem' something?"

"Well, I remember 'redeeming' stamps from the grocery store back in the day," said Maggie, one of our senior citizens. "We would collect stamps whenever we went shopping, and we would paste them into a book. Then we could 'redeem' the stamps at the redemption center for a toaster or a mixer or something, depending on how many books we turned in."

"So how would you 'redeem' a soul?" I asked her.

After a bit of a pause, Maggie said, "That's odd. I have always heard preachers say that to 'redeem' something meant to buy it back. They would talk about slaves in Bible days being redeemed when their family was able to produce enough money. Brought out of slavery, into freedom.

"Right," I said. "I've preached that sermon."

"But maybe it works just as well the other way. Before we knew Jesus, we were nothing. We were worthless. We weren't useful for anything. Like a book of cheap stamps from the grocery store."

"Fit only for the fire," I suggested.

Maggie chuckled. "I guess so. But when Jesus redeems us from sin, He turns us into something profitable. Something that will serve His purposes."

"Sounds like something worth singing about," I said.

What does "I Will Sing of My Redeemer" mean to you? _____
_____
_____
_____

The Bible Study Song List

If you were putting a list together for a study about forgiveness, what songs would you include and why? _____
_____
_____
_____

What songs might you exclude and why? _____
_____
_____

Psalm 40
A Song for the Patient

The 40th Psalm is one of several written in the same spirit as Philippians 4:6—"Don't worry about anything, but in everything, through prayer and petition with thanksgiving, let your requests be made known to God." The best way to ask favor from God is to remember the abundant favor He has already bestowed. Giving thanks helps us keep our current hardships in the proper context.

David remembers here of a time in his life where he had suffered remarkable hardship patiently. In the end, his confidence in God was vindicated, lifting him up from the unstable surroundings in which he had found himself and establishing him firmly. On that occasion, he writes in verse 3, "He put a new song in my mouth a hymn of praise to our God." Does he refer to Psalm 9, in which he credits God for the retreat of his enemies? Or perhaps Psalm 18, in which he credits God for their defeat? Or perhaps a more general song of praise to the glory of God, such as Psalm 30 or Psalm 33? On the other hand, the "song" may be figurative, or refer to a praise remaining between David and his God.

In any case, the song clearly was a result of the happiness in his heart. He turned to God in times of trouble instead of "to the proud or to those who run after lies" (v.4). After all, what could man possibly do in comparison to the power and generosity of God?

All God asks of us in return is to be able to say with David, "I delight to do Your will,

> [1] I waited patiently for the LORD,
> and He turned to me and heard my cry for help.
> [2] He brought me up from a desolate pit,
> out of the muddy clay,
> and set my feet on a rock,
> making my steps secure.
> [3] He put a new song in my mouth,
> a hymn of praise to our God.
> Many will see and fear,
> and put their trust in the LORD.
> [4] How happy is the man
> who has put his trust in the LORD
> and has not turned to the proud
> or to those who run after lies!
> [5] LORD, my God, You have done many things —
> Your wonderful works and Your plans for us;
> none can compare with You.
> If I were to report and speak of them,
> they are more than can be told.
> [6] You do not delight in sacrifice and offering;
> You open my ears to listen.
> You do not ask for a whole burnt offering or a sin offering.
> [7] Then I said, "See, I have come;
> it is written about me in the volume of the scroll.
> [8] I delight to do Your will, my God;
> Your instruction resides within me."

⁹ I proclaim righteousness in the great assembly;
see, I do not keep my mouth closed
— as You know, LORD.
¹⁰ I did not hide Your righteousness in my heart
I spoke about Your faithfulness and salvation;
I did not conceal Your constant love and truth
from the great assembly.
¹¹ LORD, do not withhold Your compassion from me;
Your constant love and truth will always guard me.
¹² For troubles without number have surrounded me;
my sins have overtaken me; I am unable to see.
They are more than the hairs of my head,
and my courage leaves me.
¹³ LORD, be pleased to deliver me;
hurry to help me, LORD.
¹⁴ Let those who seek to take my life
be disgraced and confounded.
Let those who wish me harm
be driven back and humiliated.
¹⁵ Let those who say to me, "Aha, aha!"
be horrified because of their shame.
¹⁶ Let all who seek You rejoice and be glad in You;
let those who love Your salvation continually say,
The LORD is great!"
¹⁷ I am afflicted and needy;
the Lord thinks of me.
You are my help and my deliverer;
my God, do not delay.

my God; Your instruction resides within me" (v. 8). Such devotion is far more important than any burnt offering or other outward gesture. Although such things were necessary under the Law of Moses, no amount of sacrifice can win a place in His graces. Only genuine obedience grounded in faith can.

Another immediate need prompted David to write Psalm 40, another hymn of praise to his Benefactor. Verse 11 indicates he considers himself already to have received God's compassion, love and truth, even though they had not manifested themselves yet. Because God's love is constant, David has confidence He will come again to his aid, bringing down those who would hurt him.

Remembering God has already decided to be on our side gives us hope and assurance in the day of trial. "On our side" may not mean He will deliver us in the way and timing of our choosing. But we can know He thinks of us in our need and affliction; "You are my help and my deliverer; my God, do not delay" (v.17).

1. What song do you find yourself singing when you contemplate the work of God? _____
_____
_____
_____
_____
_____
_____
_____
_____

> ## Figure of Speech
> ### The Hairs of My Head
>
> Those who are balding may take offense at this expression. But even those who are thinning can appreciate the sheer number of hair follicles atop a typical human head. Researchers put the actual number at between 100,000 and 200,000 hairs for a healthy human. Between 50 and 100 of them fall out every day, and the average person doesn't even realize it.
>
> When Jesus says, "But even the hairs of your head have all been counted" (Matthew 10:30), He is not saying that God can narrow that literal number down for us; He means that the God of heaven is intimately acquainted with our lives—more so than we are ourselves. And this is not simply because of who He is. The context before and after verse 30 speak of the place even sparrows have in His heart. And "you are worth more than many sparrows." God knows us so well because He loves us so much. Even the loss of a single hair among thousands is significant in His sight.

2. Is there a New Testament equivalent of "sacrifice and offering?" If so, how important is it to give it in the context of salvation by grace? _____
   _____
   _____
   _____
   _____

3. What form might God's salvation from difficulty take, other than the actual removal of the problem? _____
   _____
   _____
   _____

4. What is your favorite line in the psalm and why? _____
   _____
   _____
   _____

The Patient: A Bible Study

It wasn't always easy for Abraham. He was 75 when he left Haran and most of his family to travel to Canaan. Although people lived considerably longer in those days (Abraham lived to be 175, and Isaac died at 180), 75 years old would have to be considered well within the parameters of "middle age." At his age, Abraham was willing to wait for God to fulfill His promises in His time—including the promise of a son to carry on the family legacy.

He waited ten years. And that was too long for his wife, Sarah, who was then called Sarai as Abraham was called Abram. Genesis 16:2 reads, "Sarai said to Abram, 'Since the LORD has prevented me from bearing children, go to my slave; perhaps I can have children by her.' And Abram agreed to what Sarai said." The text is unclear as to whether Sarai thought having a child through Hagar would qualify as God fulfilling His promise to her husband. What is clear, though, is that she blamed God for her inability to do her part. She, and perhaps Abram as well, grew impatient with God. The birth of Ishmael followed. This birth not only fell short of God's promise, it horribly complicated their family life to the point of Abram eventually having to put Ishmael and his mother, Hagar, out of his home permanently—a heartbreaking decision for a father who truly loved his son.

They waited 13 more years. Then (and, judging from the absence of information in the text, only then) God reaffirmed His covenant with Abram by changing his and Sarah's name. "I will establish My covenant between Me and you, and I will multiply you greatly...Your name will no longer be Abram, but your name will be Abraham, for I will make you the father of many nations" (Genesis 17:2-5). By this point, Abraham also seems to doubt the promise—or at least in his mind had decided that Ishmael was the fulfillment. Although Sarah is often criticized for laughing in the face of God's promise, Abraham laughed first (Genesis 17:17). He would go on to have more children even later in life (Genesis 25:1-2). Abraham thought children at his age would be a remarkable thing. Sarah herself was almost certainly postmenopausal (Genesis 18:11-12).

As the angel said on that occasion, "Is anything impossible for the LORD?" (Genesis 18:13). God had made a promise. Although He had been a long time (as Abraham and Sarah would have defined "long"), and it no longer seemed possible for it to occur as God had said, such considerations do not limit God. Our faith should not be limited, either.

They waited one more year. This year, of course, was much easier than the others. First, they were told a specific timeframe; second, that timeframe was not excessive; third, as Sarah's pregnancy became more and more apparent, they were able to see God's promise nearing fulfillment day by day.

We don't, unfortunately. Most of God's demands on our patience do not come with an indicator of when they might end. If we can turn our waiting hours (and days, and months, and years) into an opportunity to build faith instead of doubt, we can find waiting for God—and waiting, and waiting—an exhilarating experience. Every day brings us closer to God's plan; therefore, by definition, every day is better than the last.

Read Psalm 40 again—this time with Abraham and Sarah in mind.

1. What is God's plan for us? How specific is it? How do we know what it is? __
_____
_____
_____
_____

2. How much are Abraham and Sarah to blame for coming up with the plan regarding Hagar? Are there situations in which we may need to change our approach to facilitate God's plan for our life? _____
_____
_____
_____

Psalm 25—A Parallel Study

"Turn to me and be gracious to me, for I am alone and afflicted." The words of Psalm 25:16 often sound familiar to us. We are alone in our suffering. No one understands. No one cares. We are not being surrounded by proof to the contrary, at least—and we would expect at least Christian brethren and close family and friends to be more supportive.

Others' failings with regard to their love and care for us should remain their problem. Although we would love to have outpourings of love from our fellow man, the only One we need is the only One who is faithful. By praying to Him in our hour of trial, we are reminded of the wisdom and providence of God—and His provision for us does not always meet our expectations.

Verse 14 reads, "The secret counsel of the LORD is for those who fear Him, and He reveals His covenant to them." Those who have enough faith to look to God for answers receive answers no one else gets, and that no one else would appreciate or understand. His covenant with us assures us that sinful people like us can find our way into His graces if we are humble enough to listen (v.8-9). And if we listen, we will hear His calm assurances.

1. David frequently asks for God's mercy and forgiveness in Psalm 25. How does patience work in favor of one who seeks forgiveness? _____
_____
_____
_____

2. How does God teach us His ways and paths (v.4)? _____
_____
_____
_____

3. Is keeping "His covenant and decrees" possible for one whose sin is great (v.10-11)? Explain. _____
_____
_____
_____

4. What is your favorite line in the psalm and why? _____
_____
_____
_____

The Patient: A Case Study

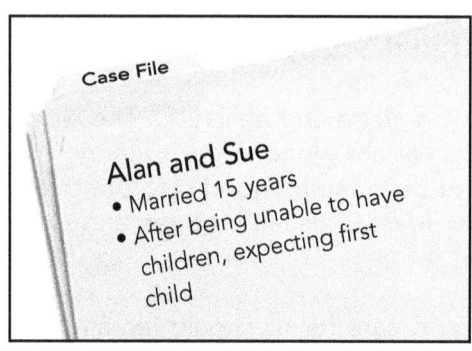

No one at church had ever seen a couple quite so giddy about a pregnancy—and that's saying something. Alan and Sue were practically bouncing off the walls with joy the day they made the announcement. After 15 years of marriage, everyone had pretty much assumed it was not going to happen for them. Her parents had even quit asking. Then suddenly, out of nowhere, came the long-awaited news.

"It's amazing how things work out," said Alan with tears in his eyes. "We wanted a child, obviously. And after a few years of trying and failing, we both went to get tested. And the doctor said we were both fine, but we had trouble conceiving for some reason. He suggested some procedures, but as you know, I have serious ethical problems with in vitro and artificial insemination. We discussed our options, and we just decided to leave it up to the Lord. If it were meant to be, it would be. And waiting as long as we did, we had pretty much decided we had gotten our answer."

"But we never quit praying about it," Sue added. "Every night, Alan would lead us—'Lord, if it is in Your will, please give us a child and the wisdom to raise it in Your care. And give us the faith to accept whatever answer you see fit to send us.' Or words to that effect."

"Are you hoping for a boy or a girl?" someone asked. Alan and Sue just turned to each other, smiled, shook their heads a bit, and hugged each other again.

Read Psalm 40 again—this time with Alan and Sue in mind.

What would you say to Alan and Sue based on Psalm 40? _____
_____
_____
_____

New Testament insight

Not one person who waits for You
will be disgraced;
those who act treacherously without cause
will be disgraced. — Psalm 25:3

Waiting on the Lord takes on a whole new meaning in a New Testament context. Paul tells the brethren in 1 Corinthians 1:7, "you do not lack any spiritual gift as you eagerly wait for the revelation of our Lord Jesus Christ." The manifestations of the Spirit that are discussed in chapters 12-14 were sufficient, Paul says, to give them the spiritual strength they needed to confront sin. The time was coming, as he argues in chapter 15, that the waiting would be over. Jesus was coming again. The "revelation" of Christ would mean life from the dead (v.13-14), purpose for our hope (v.19), and ultimate defeat of death itself (v.26).

Those same gifts, now preserved for us in written form, strengthen us as we wait as well. We may very well be moved to doubt His return, as in God's wisdom the day continues to delay. We are reminded in 2 Peter 3:8-9, though, that His delay is more a product of His mercy than His hesitation. And as Peter points out earlier in the chapter, those who doubt He will destroy the world should remember that He has already done it once. His promise is sure.

"Therefore, my dear brothers, be steadfast, immovable, always excelling in the Lord's work, knowing that your labor in the Lord is not in vain" (1 Corinthians 15:48).

The Patient: A Hymn Study

Adelaide Pollard was a hymn writer who had hopes of traveling to Africa for missionary work but was discouraged at her inability to raise the needed funds. She attended a prayer service one evening during that time, and she heard an elderly woman say in prayer, "It really doesn't matter what you do with us, Lord, just have Your own way with our lives." The sentiment resonated with Pollard. Considering the statement, especially in consideration of Jeremiah 18:3 and the prophet's analogy of the potter and clay, she penned all four stanzas of "Have

Have Thine Own Way, Lord

Words: Adelaide A. Pollard
Music: George C. Stebbins

Thine Own Way, Lord," that evening. She wrote many hymns in her life but attached her name to very few. "Have Thine Own Way, Lord" is the only one in common usage today.

George Coles Stebbins supplied the music five years later. Stebbins, known across American in his day for his work with D.L. Moody's evangelistic crusades, is perhaps best known today for his collaborations with Fanny J. Crosby ("Truehearted, Wholehearted," "Jesus is Tenderly Calling," "Some Day the Silver Cord Will Break").

"Have Thine Own Way, Lord" went on to be an extremely popular hymn, being recorded by Mahalia Jackson, Marty Robbins, Johnny Cash, Jim Reeves, and by Ronnie Milsap on his 2009 gospel album, *Then Sings My Soul*.

And yes, Adelaide Pollard did eventually find her way to Africa.

The Patient: A Worship Study

There are several excellent hymns addressing the topic of patience in the Lord—"In His Time," "Teach Me, Lord, to Wait," "The Lord is My Light" (my favorite of the bunch), and, of course, "Have Thine Own Way," which we saved for last.

Archer spoke first afterward. "That's what patience is all about, isn't it? Waiting for the Lord to do His business."

"Exactly," I said. "And more than that—waiting for Him, and believing His way is going to be the right way, no matter what it is or how long it takes."

"I think that's the challenge," said Archer's wife, Sandra. "We can all wait. In fact, we have to wait. We don't have a choice. We can ask God to speed things up, and often we do, but we don't have any real control. God will do what He will do. He arrives when he arrives.

"The trick is waiting with the right attitude. Not thinking He has forgotten about us. Not thinking we have to come up with a Plan B on our own that conflicts with His will. Genuinely believing God is in control and all we have to do is trust in Him, keep praising, quit whining."

"It's in that last line in the first stanza—'While I am waiting, yielded and still,'" Archer added. "God is making something in us, with us. The more we devote ourselves to Him and His word, the more we let Him change us. But it doesn't happen overnight. And that can be very discouraging."

"Thankfully, God is more patient with us than we are sometimes with ourselves," I said. Amens followed.

What does "Have Thine Own Way, Lord" mean to you?
_____
_____
_____

The Bible Study Song List

If you were putting a list together for a study about patience, what songs would you include and why? _____
_____
_____

What songs about shepherds might you exclude and why? _____
_____
_____
_____

Psalm 42
A Song for the Depressed

Why am I so depressed?

We have all asked ourselves that question at some point and come away frustrated. And depressed.

Depression makes no sense for the Christian. After all, we have Jesus. We have the hope of heaven. We have the Spirit, who guides us through the inspired word (John 14:15-18; 2 Peter 1:19-21). We know the hardships of this life are temporary and heaven is eternal. We know all these things. We are reminded of them constantly. We remind ourselves constantly. And yet…

Why am I so depressed?

Just telling ourselves to "snap out of it" won't work any better than it does for others when we tell them the same thing. Perhaps searching for a way to feel better in the short term is the wrong approach. The objective should not be to put a smile on our face; it should be to draw closer to God.

The psalmist feels a craving for God in his times of despair; "As a deer longs for streams of water, so I long for You, God" (v.1). His neighbors expect his God to come to his rescue and are surprised when He doesn't — or, if you read verse 3 more as a rebuke (as it clearly is in verse 10), they mock him for holding to a faith that doesn't work.

Clinical depression, which is an actual medical condition that may require medical treatment, is different from what most people suffer from time to time—a stubborn inability to emerge

[1] As a deer longs for streams of water,
so I long for You, God.
[2] I thirst for God, the living God.
When can I come and appear before God?
[3] My tears have been my food day and night,
while all day long people say to me,
"Where is your God?"
[4] I remember this as I pour out my heart:
how I walked with many,
leading the festive procession to the house of God,
with joyful and thankful shouts.
[5] Why am I so depressed?
Why this turmoil within me?
Put your hope in God, for I will still praise Him,
my Savior and my God.
[6] I am deeply depressed;
therefore I remember You from the land of Jordan
and the peaks of Hermon,
from Mount Mizar.
[7] Deep calls to deep in the roar of Your waterfalls;
all Your breakers and Your billows have swept over me.

⁸ The LORD will send His faithful love by day;
His song will be with me in the night—
a prayer to the God of my life.
⁹ I will say to God, my rock, "Why have You forgotten me? Why must I go about in sorrow
because of the enemy's oppression?"
¹⁰ My adversaries taunt me, as if crushing my bones,
while all day long they say to me,
"Where is your God?"
¹¹ Why am I so depressed? Why this turmoil within me?
Put your hope in God, for I will still praise Him,
my Savior and my God.

from a sad, bored or lethargic state of mind. People suffering from ordinary, garden-variety depression can convince themselves that life cannot go on normally until the depression goes away; and when it doesn't, it only gets that much worse.

Why am I so depressed?

The psalmist asks and asks and asks. But he does not allow his bad mood— whatever caused it, however long it lasts—to alter his routine. He certainly does not change his commitment to God. He keeps praying. He keeps worshiping. And yes, he keeps searching for a way out of the doldrums. Through it all, he says, "Put your hope in God, for I will still praise Him" (v.11). Surely a faithful child of God who persists in his faith, who sees depression as something to be dealt with instead of wallowed in, will with God's help come out on the other side in time—and stronger for the effort.

Twice in the psalm our Father is referred to as "my Savior and my God." If we believe Him to be the One who spoke all things into existence, in whom "we live and move and exist" (Acts 17:28)—surely we can believe that, in His time and in His way, He will be our Savior as well.

1. Is it God's job to make us more contented with life? Explain. _____
   _____
   _____
   _____
   _____

2. Is it possible to be "leading the festive procession to the house of God, with joyful and thankful shouts" (v.4) while we are depressed? If so, how? _____
   _____
   _____
   _____

> ### Figure of Speech
>
> ### Deep Calls to Deep
>
> "Deep" used as a noun in the Bible generally refers to deep waters (Genesis 1:2; Job 28:14), particularly waters threatening to overwhelm a person (Jonah 2:3). In the context of Psalm 42:7, the meaning seems to be that the sound of God's waterfalls, breakers and billows echo one upon another, showing constant and increasing trouble for him.
>
> The overall context, not only of hardship and fear but also of triumphant faith, leaves open the possibility that a secondary, hopeful meaning is also there. In the previous verse we read, "I am deeply depressed; therefore I remember You." The deep emotional burden being carried is countered by an even deeper commitment from God toward His child.
>
> "The LORD will send His faithful love by day" (v.8). As deep as our troubles may be, as impossible as it may seem to emerge from them, the Father's love for us is even deeper. We can have confidence He will ultimately lift us up to heights unimaginable if we do not lose faith in time of doubt.

3. At what point does depression become selfish? Explain. _____
   _____
   _____
   _____

4. What is your favorite line in the psalm and why? _____
   _____
   _____
   _____

The Depressed: A Bible Study

The name "Naomi" means "pleasant." Nothing in the book of Ruth indicates she was not aptly named in the early part of her life. She had a husband, a livelihood, and two sons. It would have been easy to see the blessings of God in those days.

Then things changed. A famine came into the land, and her husband Elimelech was forced to move the family to Moab, away from their family and friends. Elimelech died. Her sons married Moabite women; that must have caused her some discomfort, even though Ruth and Orpah both appear devoted to her.

Then Mahlon and Chilion died, childless. Virtually everything she had ever called her own was gone.

Finding no consolation among outsiders, she determined to return to Bethlehem and find whatever living she might there among her kinsmen. Although it is easy to criticize Naomi for her poor attitude, those who have suffered loss can relate to her when she rejected her "pleasant" name for one meaning "bitter."

"Don't call me Naomi. Call me Mara," she answered, "for the Almighty has made me very bitter. I left full, but the LORD has brought me back empty. Why do you call me Naomi, since the LORD has pronounced judgment on me, and the Almighty has afflicted me?" (Ruth 1:20-21).

Anyone who has gotten used to pleasant, sweet food and suddenly tastes bitterness understands Naomi's plight. Having everything you want makes it all the more difficult if you are forced to have nothing. And if we are used to crediting God for the blessings of life, it could become easy to blame Him, as Naomi did, for the hardships.

In Naomi's grief (and likely a bit of self-pity), she got a few things wrong. One, God doesn't make a person bitter; we choose bitterness for ourselves. Others (David in 2 Samuel 12:21-23, for instance) can find enough faith to strengthen their attachment to God instead of lashing out at Him; if they can do it, we can do it as well. Two, she had a host of relatives and distant neighbors who appear to have been genuinely excited to see her return home; such ones can be a tremendous blessing to us when dealing with grief—until and unless we push them away with our poor attitude.

Most notably of all, though, is her failure to appreciate the blessing God had given her in her daughter-in-law, Ruth. Naomi must have had a tremendous influence on Ruth during their years together—enough for Ruth to abandon all she had ever known and attach herself to a foreign woman and the foreign God she served. Because Ruth was willing to love and support Naomi even through Naomi's bitter days, Ruth was in a position to provide a living for herself and Naomi gleaning in the fields of Boaz. And Naomi was motivated to guide her actions in the days that followed, bringing blessings to herself and Ruth. Surely this is a sign that she was learning to put aside her bitterness—at least enough to act responsibly for herself and others.

If Ruth had not been faithful to Naomi, Naomi likely would have suffered greatly in her declining years; Ruth herself may have remained widowed and childless, and almost certainly would not have come to properly know and serve the God of heaven. If Naomi had thought only of herself, as excessively bitter people often do, she would not have been alert enough to help form a marriage between Ruth and Boaz; the barren future for her family that she anticipated would have become a reality.

Instead, Ruth found another husband and another family. God blessed Naomi with a grandson who himself would be the grandfather of the greatest king of all (Ruth 4:17). Most importantly, God providentially kept the genealogical line moving forward, leading eventually to the birth of Jesus Christ Himself (Matthew 1:1, 5).

Blessings come in odd places and odd pathways. For Naomi, having a daughter—and her only by marriage—turned out to be more of a blessing than having two sons.

Read Psalm 42 again — this time with Naomi in mind.

1. What are we trying to accomplish when we blame God for our difficulties? __
   _____
   _____
   _____
   _____

2. How much patience should be expected from someone who is trying to help an embittered friend or relative? Contrast this with the responsibility of the embittered one to improve their own attitude. _____
   _____
   _____
   _____

Psalm 22—A Parallel Study

Jesus knew the Scriptures intimately; His decision to reflect verbally and specifically on Psalm 22 was no accident. All of God's faithful ones occasionally find themselves asking why God's presence is not seen or felt, why His deliverance for which we wait is so long in coming.

The images of affliction abound in Psalm 22. "I am a worm" (v.6). "I am poured out like water" (v.14). "My strength is dried up like baked clay" (v.15). Many of them, including pierced hands and feet (v.16), seem almost specific to Jesus; John 19:24 quotes verse 18 as being fulfilled in Jesus. Worst of all, suffering is used by evildoers to argue that the one in pain is not righteous. "He relies on the LORD; let Him rescue him" (v.8)—almost precisely what Jesus' tormentors said at the cross (Matthew 27:43).

Just as Jesus was able to endure the cross and emerge victoriously, so also we can know He hears our pleas, continues to love us, and offers deliverance—even if it doesn't come exactly the way we would have chosen.

1. How many parallels can you find between David's suffering and Jesus' suffering on the cross? _____
_____
_____
_____

2. In what sense is God ruling over the nations (v.28)? _____
_____
_____
_____

3. "Even the one who cannot preserve his life" (v.29) must submit to God. Name some examples of those who continued in faith despite imminent death. ____
_____
_____
_____

4. What is your favorite line in the psalm and why? _____
_____
_____
_____

New Testament Insight

My God, My God, why have you forsaken me? — Psalm 22:1

Was Jesus truly "forsaken" on the cross? It seems impossible. How could God cease to be in fellowship with God?

Understanding Psalm 22 and its connection to Jesus on the cross helps considerably. The figurative depictions of David's afflictions (pierced hands and feet, gambling for his clothing, and particularly the quotation in verse 8 that is unwittingly referenced by Jesus' malefactors in Matthew 27:43) are actually, on a deeper level, Messianic prophecies. When Jesus quoted verse 1 from the cross (Matthew 27:46, Mark 15:34), He was telling those present, as well as us, what was on His mind at the time; more than that, He was acknowledging Himself as the deeper fulfillment of the text.

As Psalm 22 makes quite evident, God does not abandon His faithful ones. After venting his frustrations that naturally occur in the minds of even the most devoted followers of God, David confirms the faithfulness of God in the final verses of the text. Verse 24 is especially relevant: "For He has not despised or detested the torment of the afflicted. He did not hide His face from him, but listened when he cried to Him for help."

God did not forsake David in his trials. He did not forsake Jesus on the cross. He will not abandon us in our time of need either—not even when it seems He already has.

The Depressed: A Case Study

Life just hadn't worked out for Jeffery. He was a nice enough guy, smart enough, good looking enough. If you had told him and his friends 20 years earlier he would be alone in his 40s, they wouldn't have believed it. He had plenty of dates, even a couple of relatively serious relationships. But he had held out for the right girl (as he imagined her to be). The right girl had not come along.

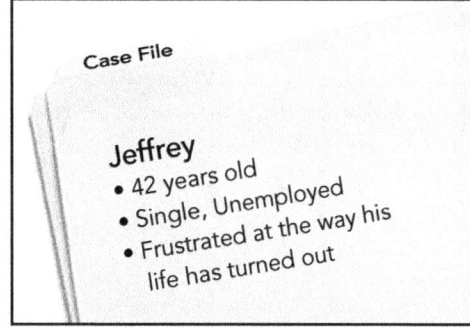

Case File

Jeffrey
- 42 years old
- Single, Unemployed
- Frustrated at the way his life has turned out

His career path was a disappointment, too. After earning a degree in computer science and getting a good job, he grew disenchanted with management and decided to start over at the bottom with a new company. That position looked promising—until the turn in the economy downsized his job. So he decided to go his own way, starting his own computer tech company. He exhausted his savings quickly, even after moving back in with his parents. Ultimately, when it seemed obvious the company was going nowhere, he decided (with his parents' help) to start over with a new degree and a new field. An MBA was next. However, jobs continued to elude him—as did the right girl.

"Some folks have all the luck," he said to a buddy in the church foyer upon hearing of another couple getting engaged. "Honestly, sometimes I think God has it in for me."

"What do you mean?"

"I mean, I'm a good Christian. I play by the rules. I treat people nicely. There are plenty of people out there with less going for them than me. But I can't ever catch a break. When does it get to be my time? When will something go my way for a change?"

Read Psalm 42 again—this time with Jeffrey in mind.

What would you say to Jeffery based on Psalm 42? _____
_____
_____
_____

Be Still, My Soul

1. Be still, my soul: the Lord is on thy side.
   Bear patient-ly the cross of grief or pain.
   Leave to thy God to or-der and pro-vide;
2. Be still, my soul: thy God doth un-der-take
   To guide the fu-ture, as He has the past.
   Thy hope, thy con-fi-dence let noth-ing shake;
3. Be still, my soul: when dear-est friends de-part,
   And all is dark-ened in the vale of tears,
   Then shalt thou bet-ter know His love, His heart,
4. Be still, my soul: the hour is has-tening on
   When we shall be for-ev-er with the Lord.
   When dis-ap-point-ment, grief and fear are gone,
5. Be still, my soul: be-gin the song of praise
   On earth, be-liev-ing, to Thy Lord on high;
   Ac-knowl-edge Him in all thy words and ways,

Psalm 42—A Song for Depressed | 49

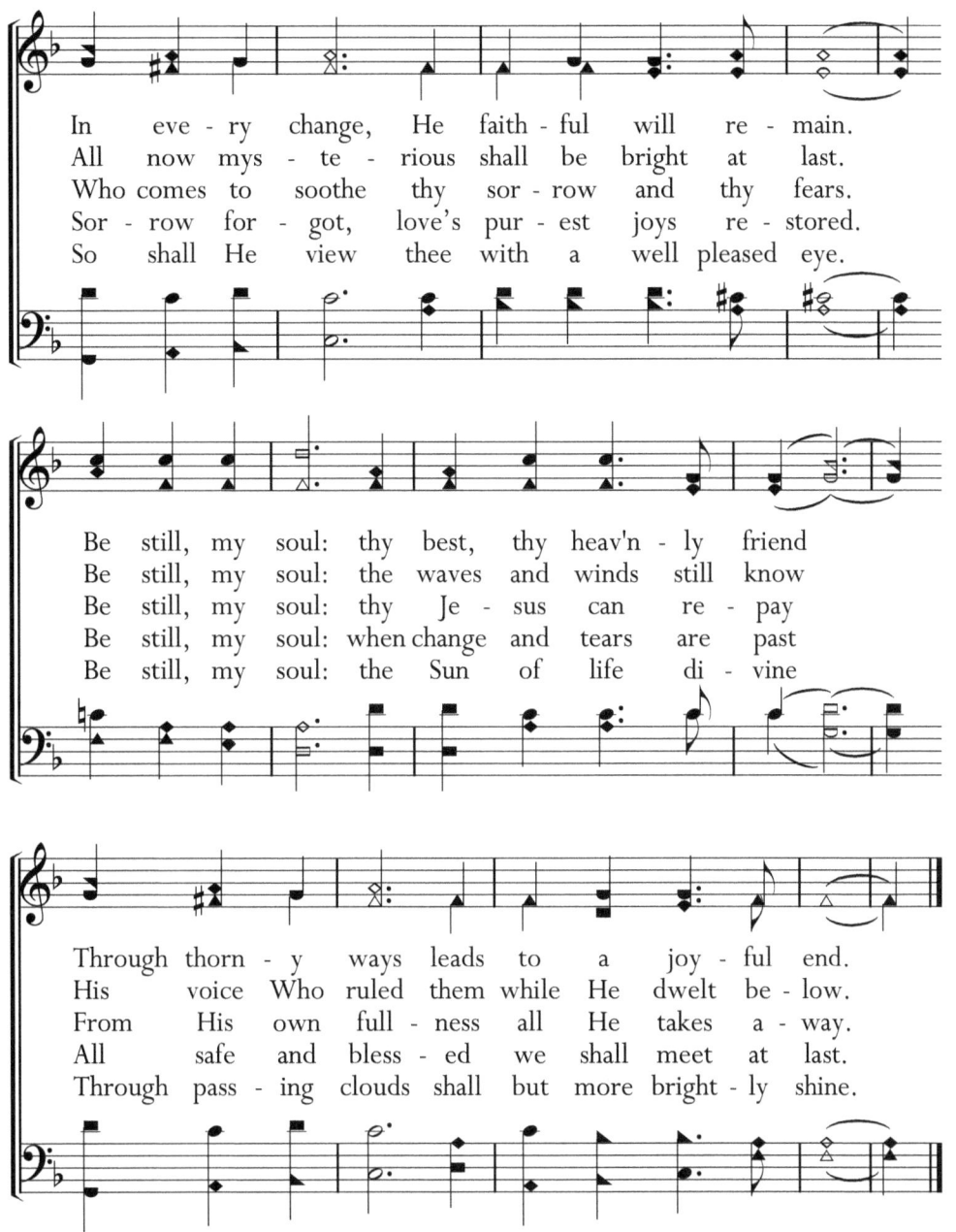

In eve-ry change, He faith-ful will re-main.
All now mys-te-rious shall be bright at last.
Who comes to soothe thy sor-row and thy fears.
Sor-row for-got, love's pur-est joys re-stored.
So shall He view thee with a well pleased eye.

Be still, my soul: thy best, thy heav'n-ly friend
Be still, my soul: the waves and winds still know
Be still, my soul: thy Je-sus can re-pay
Be still, my soul: when change and tears are past
Be still, my soul: the Sun of life di-vine

Through thorn-y ways leads to a joy-ful end.
His voice Who ruled them while He dwelt be-low.
From His own full-ness all He takes a-way.
All safe and bless-ed we shall meet at last.
Through pass-ing clouds shall but more bright-ly shine.

Words: Katherine von Sclegel, Tr. Jane L. Borthwick
Music: Jean Sibelius

F - 2 - MI

The Depressed: A Hymn Study

"Be Still, My Soul," was written by Katherine von Schlegel during the height of the Pietistic revival in Germany. This movement encouraged evangelism and religious fervor much as did the Puritan and Wesleyan movements in England. Little is known of von Schlegel other than she was a Lutheran woman who wrote and published several religious lyrics, including extra verses to "Be Still, My Soul" seldom sung. She died around 1768. About a hundred years later, her hymn was translated into English by Jane L. Borthwick, a devoted worker in the Free Church of Scotland.

Finlandia Hymn is a name associated with part of the symphonic poem Finlandia by Jean Sibelius. Sibelius reworked the section into a stand-alone piece recognized as an important nationalistic song in Finland, Sibelius' homeland. The music has been used for multiple hymns over the centuries, including "Be Still, My Soul." In 2007, the Brigham Young University Men's Choir recorded a song called "The Psalm of Nephi," with words adapted from the Book of Mormon, 2 Nephi 4:16-35. It was also adopted as the tune for the national anthem of Biafra, "Land of the Rising Sun," during its attempted secession from Nigeria.

"Be Still, My Soul" was reportedly the favorite hymn of Eric Liddle, the Scottish missionary who gained fame by refusing to compete on a Sunday in the 1924 Olympic Games in Paris, as detailed in the film Chariots of Fire. Liddle is said to have taught the hymn to his fellow prisoners in the World War II prison camp in China where he was detained and eventually died.

The Depressed: A Worship Study

"It's interesting to me that we should focus on 'Be Still, My Soul' in a lesson on depression," said Natalie, one of our teenagers. "Personally, I find that song extremely depressing. I know it has a good message and all that, and the message is the most important part of the song. Still, you know what I mean."

"Do you think it's just too slow?" I asked.

"That's part of it. And the bit about bearing 'the cross of grief or pain.'"

"Well, what do you think that 'cross' is?" I asked.

"The price of discipleship. We serve Jesus at a cost. I understand that. Still, I'm not getting any benefit from singing about it."

"I get that. And you may be right as far as the meaning of the hymn goes. But personally, I think "the cross of grief or pain" is the burden we all bear in life. 'We all have our crosses to bear,' right? But when Jesus is our Lord, the cross gets easier. Galatians 6:2 tells us we have brothers and sisters in Christ who are there to help us carry our burdens. That's a blessing from God. And we have prayer to help us—1 Peter 5:7 tells us to cast all our cares on God.

"'Thy hope, thy confidence let nothing shake.' Hard times will come, even when we are Christians. But when we have faith, we know 'thy heavenly Friend, thru thorny ways leads to a joyful end.' We just have to be still. Quit our fussing. Let Him take control. Trust Him to give us what we need, and the strength to cope with what we don't want."

What does "Be Still, My Soul" mean to you? _____
_____
_____

The Bible Study Song List

If you were putting a list together for a study about depression, what songs would you include and why? _____
_____
_____

What songs might you exclude and why? _____
_____
_____

Psalm 46
A Song for the Fearful

The student of the Bible will have trouble reading Psalm 46 without thinking of the story of Noah and the flood. Faith compelled Noah and his family to board the ark. Faith persuaded them that doing so would protect them from the certain destruction and devastation to come. Although the text says nothing about it, we cannot help but suspect that fear crept into the hearts of more than one of the eight preserved souls. During the time on the ark (more than a year in total), they were sequestered from all they had ever known and were at the mercy of the winds and waves busy destroying the entire planet.

The world Noah's family eventually stepped out into was dramatically changed, as would necessarily be the case after a global flood. As they considered the coming changes, and eventually as they accepted the changes that had happened, they could draw strength from the one thing that had not and would not ever change—God Himself.

Ironically, God is portrayed in terms of water as He comes to the aid of those threatened by roaring and foaming waters. The gracious flow from heaven is only a threat to God's enemies. Whatever destruction comes from His throne is ultimately a blessing to those who put their confidence in Him.

As mankind squabbles over issues ranging from traffic infractions to wholesale genocide—each side in each conflict convinced of its righteousness—God asserts His authority. "Stop your fighting," He says. Quit acting as though your personal causes are the end-all be-all of existence. Promoting such causes,

> [1] God is our refuge and strength,
> a helper who is always found in times of trouble.
> [2] Therefore we will not be afraid,
> though the earth trembles and the mountains topple into the depths of the seas,
> [3] though its waters roar and foam
> and the mountains quake with its turmoil.
> [4] There is a river—
> its streams delight the city of God,
> the holy dwelling place of the Most High.
> [5] God is within her; she will not be toppled.
> God will help her when the morning dawns.
> [6] Nations rage, kingdoms topple;
> the earth melts when He lifts His voice.

and enforcing them with whatever bows and spears we might be able to bring to bear, denies the supremacy of the God who made all such things.

Living in a world characterized by such conflict can become terrifying. The key is to trust in God—to fear Him more than we fear the things in the world. Proverbs 1:7, and many other passages besides, reads "The fear of the LORD is the beginning of knowledge."

⁷ The LORD of Hosts is with us;
the God of Jacob is our
stronghold. *Selah*
⁸ Come, see the works of the
LORD,
who brings devastation on
the earth.
⁹ He makes wars cease
throughout the earth.
He shatters bows and cuts
spears to pieces;
He burns up the chariots.
¹⁰ "Stop your fighting—and
know that I am God,
exalted among the nations,
exalted on the earth."
¹¹ The LORD of Hosts is with us;
the God of Jacob is our
stronghold.

1. What are we most afraid of in this life? What is God's answer? _____
_____
_____
_____
_____

2. What are some circumstances we face today in which the earth might be seen figuratively as "trembling?" How does God allay our fears in such times? _____
_____
_____
_____
_____
_____

3. What sort of fighting are we to stop when considering the nature and authority of God? _____
_____
_____
_____
_____

4. What is your favorite line in the psalm and why? _____
_____
_____
_____
_____
_____
_____

> ### Figure of Speech
>
> **"He Makes Wars Cease"**
>
> Whatever conflicts were occurring among men at the time of the flood, apparently they were stopped. When the time for God to destroy the world comes again, this time by fire (2 Peter 3:10), whatever conflicts are ongoing then will be stopped as well. Nothing goes on in this world without God's permission; and as patient as He is with our bickering and selfish pride, He will put a stop to it one day.
>
> In a figurative sense, "He makes wars cease" even today. Isaiah 11:1-10 prefigures the gospel age. Enemies such as wolf and lamb will coexist in peace. This passage looks forward to the time the revelation of "the mystery of the Messiah"—that "the Gentiles are co-heirs [with the Jews], members of the same body, and partners of the promise in Christ Jesus through the gospel" (Ephesians 3:4-6). We find opportunities to fight when we focus on our differences. Coming together to honor "the LORD of hosts," we ignore our petty issues and rejoice in our common salvation.

The Fearful: A Bible Study

The numbers we read in the Bible can be staggering. In 2 Chronicles 14:8, we read King Asa had an army totaling 580,000 men. Even if you factor in "round numbers," you cannot escape the conclusion that virtually every able-bodied man in Judah and Benjamin must have been mustered for service. It was not nearly enough; the invading army of Cushites outnumbered Asa's forces almost two to one. They were equipped with chariots, an advanced form of weaponry the Israelites were slow to adopt. It must have been terrifying.

Asa was a man of faith. He committed himself to the task of defending his nation, God's nation. On the eve of doing so, he prayed what must have been the most fervent prayer of his righteous life: "LORD, there is no one besides You to help the mighty and those without strength. Help us, LORD our God, for we depend on You, and in Your name we have come against this multitude. LORD, You are our God. Do not let a mere mortal hinder You" (2 Chronicles 14:11).

The results should surprise no one who believes in the God of heaven. Not only were the Cushites routed, but they were also "crushed before the LORD and before His army. So the people of Judah carried off a great supply of loot" (2 Chronicles 14:13). A time of certain doom turned into a time of tremendous blessing and victory—all because a faithful king retreated toward God in a dire circumstance rather than retreating away from Him.

Read Psalm 46 again—this time with Asa in mind.

1. Is a fight to which we attach God's name necessarily a fight God will empower us to win? Explain. _____
_____
_____
_____

2. Read about the rest of Asa's reign as king. Did fear re-emerge, and did he continue to trust in God? _____
_____
_____
_____

Psalm 56—A Parallel Study

Everyone gets afraid of something at some point. God is aware of our predicament. He is even said in verse 8 to keep and store the tears we cry. He is intimately acquainted with all of our enemies and hardships, and He has given us His word that He will deliver us. Therefore, as David writes in verse 11, "in God I trust; I will not fear. What can man do to me?"

Submitting ourselves to God, even in the heat of the moment, constitutes a binding vow. If we trust Him to deliver us, we are obligated to follow through with our commitment to Him. It would be the height of ingratitude to accept all the blessings God gives us when we promise to follow Him and then go about our business as though nothing has changed. Everything changes when we commit to God, or else a wrath far worse than our earthly enemies could manage will come upon us.

1. What kind of things make us afraid in this life? How does God offer us help?
_____
_____
_____
_____

2. List the ways in which evil people are said to oppress the man of God. _____
_____
_____
_____

3. The title of Psalm 56 indicates it is set "when the Philistines seized him in Gath." Find the passage in which this event occurs and summarize the story. _____
_____
_____
_____

4. What is your favorite line in the psalm and why? _____
_____
_____
_____

The Fearful: A Case Study

"You know we love you and Allison," the elders said to Arthur, the local preacher with the congregation for the previous ten years. "You have done great work for us, and we don't want to minimize any of it. We want you to stay here as long as you are willing. We want to be clear on that point."

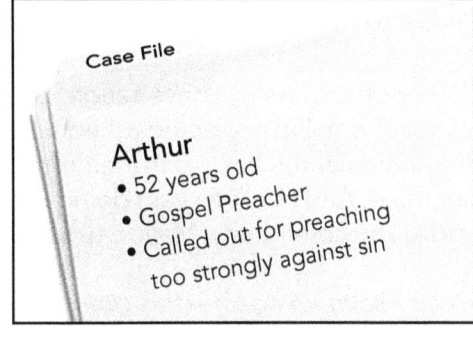

Case File

Arthur
- 52 years old
- Gospel Preacher
- Called out for preaching too strongly against sin

Arthur, knowing where the conversation was going, nodded. One of the elders had a daughter who was going through a messy divorce and had taken a recent sermon of Arthur's on Matthew 19 personally.

The particular elder, in fact, was the one doing most of the talking. "I think we are going to have to agree to disagree on our application of Jesus' marriage principles. You want to make His prohibition on divorce and remarriage apply to everyone in every case, and I'm just not sure that's a fair treatment of the text. I respect your point of view and your knowledge of the Scriptures. But we've talked, and we just don't want to be quite that closed-minded about it."

"This is the same point of view I have held from the pulpit ever since I came here," Arthur responded. "It's the same point of view I fleshed out—at the elders' request, by the way—before I was ever invited to be a part of the work here. Half of you gentlemen were already serving as elders at that time. You all nodded your heads. You all agreed with me. So what has changed in ten years? I haven't changed. Jesus hasn't changed. The Bible hasn't changed. Only the eldership has changed. I can't help thinking individual circumstances and loyalties have taken your eyes off the ball here."

"There's no need to get personal about this," said the elder in question again, irritated. "This is not just about one elder, or one woman, or one marriage. We are talking about potentially forcing Christians out of our fellowship, basically forcing them to join up with a congregation somewhere else in the area that probably doesn't stand for the truth."

("That's ironic," Arthur said to himself.)

"We didn't bring you here to debate the point," said another elder—one who had served for almost 20 years and who had been instrumental in bringing Arthur to the work initially. "We understand your point of view, and we respect it. We're not saying you're wrong. But we are not going to allow the church to be torn up over this. Are you going to let this go, or not?"

"What am I supposed to do?" Arthur asked a trusted preaching colleague over the phone that night. "I have two boys in the local college. All their friends are here. My wife has a job here. I can't just uproot us all and head out for who knows where.

"The bottom line is, I have taught the truth on this issue. I've delivered my soul on that front. I'm not being asked to teach anything false. And the elders are the shepherds of the flock; it is their responsibility to guide the church, ultimately—not mine. And I believe I am doing great work here, both with the local members and in the community. Maybe this is something I just need to learn to live with."

Read Psalm 46 again—this time with Arthur in mind.

What would you say to Arthur based on Psalm 46? _____
_____
_____
_____

New Testament Insight

> *There is a river—*
> *its streams delight the city of God,*
> *the holy dwelling place of the Most High.* — Psalm 46:4

As was noted in the lesson on Psalm 1, the image of a river connotes constant refreshment, constant care. A river (especially in times past, before the days of modern dams and irrigation systems) could be counted on year after year to bring water to the land that needed it and to the people who lived on that land.

Part of the description of the glorified people of God is the image of "the river of living water, sparkling like crystal, flowing from the throne of God and of the Lamb down the middle of the broad street of the city. On both sides of the river was the tree of life bearing 12 kinds of fruit, producing its fruit every month" (Revelation 22:1-2). The idea of a river running down Main Street, as it were, or a tree growing in the middle of a river may be odd to us, but the message is clear: God provides life for His people, and He will sustain the life forever.

Some take Revelation 22 to be describing our heavenly home, to be revealed in glory. Some take words such as those in Revelation 1:3 ("the time is near") more literally and believe it is the glorious church, rejoicing in the eventual downfall of its enemies here on earth. In either case, "the Holy City, new Jerusalem" (Revelation 21:2) is a place of glorious and eternal refreshment in the presence of God.

The Fearful: A Hymn Study

"Eternal Father, Strong to Save" is often known as "The Navy Hymn." An Englishman named William Whiting, who at the age of 35 felt God spared his life when a storm struck a ship on which he was traveling, wrote the hymn. He is thought to have drawn inspiration from Psalm 107 and its images of storms and ships. Whiting wrote four verses—the first addressing the Father, the second the Son, the third the Holy Spirit, the fourth all three.

Within a year of its writing, "Eternal Father, Strong to Save" appeared in the influential hymnal *Hymns Ancient and Modern*, in which included several added changes to the text—most of which were approved by Whiting in later versions of the hymn. John Bacchus Dykes, an Anglican clergyman, penned the music to this and about 300 other hymns, including "Holy, Holy, Holy" and "Lead, Kindly Light." He named this tune "Melita," after the archaic name for Malta, the island in the Mediterranean Sea on which the apostle Paul suffered shipwreck (Acts 27:31-28:1).

By the late 1800s, the hymn had been adopted for standard use by both British and American navies. Over the years, variations have been produced to ask specifically God's blessings for particular groups such as the Marines, the Coast Guard, SEALs, Navy fliers, astronauts and female sailors. The Episcopal church specifically altered the hymn in their official hymnals to create a version invoking God's blessings upon those on the land and in the air as well as on the sea.

The hymn has a long and storied history of usage. It was sung at Winston Churchill's request aboard the HMS *Prince of Wales* on August 9, 1941, at the conference that created the Atlantic Charter. It is commonly used at funerals, especially for those who were affiliated with the U.S. Navy; Franklin Roosevelt, John F. Kennedy and Gerald Ford are a handful of notable examples. It was played at the memorial service conducted for those who died on the USS *Maine* at the beginning of the Spanish-American War in February 1898, and to honor those killed on the USS *Cole*, which was bombed by terrorists in the Yemeni port of Aden on October 12, 2000.

Eternal Father, Strong to Save

1. E-ter-nal Fa-ther, strong to save, Whose arm hath bound the rest-less wave, Who bidd'st the might-y o-cean deep Its own ap-point-ed lim-its keep: O, hear us when we cry to Thee, For those in per-il on the sea!

2. O Christ! Whose voice the wa-ters heard And hushed their rag-ing at Thy Word, Who walk-edst on the foam-ing deep, And calm a-midst its rage did sleep; O, hear us when we cry to Thee, For those in per-il on the sea!

3. Al-might-y God of love and pow'r! Our breth-ren shield in dan-ger's hour; From rock and tem-pest, fire and foe, Pro-tect them where-so-e'er they go; Thus ev-er-more shall rise to Thee Glad hymns of praise from land and sea.

Words: William Whiting
Music: John B. Dykes

C-4-DO

The Fearful: A Worship Study

Alice was putting up a good front, but it wasn't any mystery about where her mind was. Her husband, a Navy SEAL, was going back on active duty; he had shipped out to a combat zone that week. Previous deployments had not put him in harm's way, but there was every reason to believe that this one was going to be different.

The subject for the study had been her idea. The day after Scott deployed, with our monthly class scheduled for the next Friday night, she called me and asked if we could skip ahead to the lesson we had planned around the hymn "Eternal Father, Strong to Save." Under the circumstances, the whole class was happy to oblige her.

After studying about duty, responsibility, just causes, and the occasional extreme consequence that comes with service, she politely excused herself into a nearby room while we sang. I'm not sure the rest of us were any more composed than she was.

"I guess it's the price you pay for marrying a SEAL," she said. "I couldn't be prouder of him. I knew who he was when I married him. His love of country and his courage were a big reason I fell in love with him in the first place. And I always knew the time would probably come when he would be called upon to put his life on the line. But now that it's real, it's almost more than I can stand.

"I mean, what if something happens? We just started our life together. I know it's not right for me to question God, to demand special favors from Him, to expect things are going to work out perfectly for us when I know perfectly well it will go very badly for someone—maybe someone who isn't right with God. But is it wrong for me to want special treatment? Because I don't know if I could handle losing him."

"That's why we pray," I said. "We pray for the strength to handle whatever comes, not just for a good outcome. 'The intense prayer of the righteous is very powerful,' says James 5:16. The more strength we need, the more we ask for, the more we get."

Smiling through tears, she said, "I don't think 'intense prayer' is going to be a problem with me for a while."

Before the group broke up, I handed her a framed picture of a navy vessel that we had made for the occasion, along with a card we had all signed. "I don't know if you are aware," I said, "but people have written special verses for 'Eternal Father' that correspond to the various branches of the military. Some have even been written for individual units. This picture has the verse written for the SEALs."

She read it aloud, with tears in her eyes. We listened, with tears in ours.

Eternal Father, faithful friend,
Be swift to answer those we send
In brotherhood and faithful trust
On hidden missions dangerous.
O hear us when we cry to Thee
For SEALs in air, on land, and sea.

What does "*Eternal Father, Strong to Save*" mean to you? _____
_____
_____
_____

The Bible Study Song List

If you were putting a list together for a study about fear, what songs would you include and why? _____
_____
_____

What songs might you exclude and why? _____
_____
_____

Psalm 49
A Song for the Wealthy

If you are reading this book, you are almost certainly wealthy by any worldly standard. In the first place, it is written in English—my only language, and a language spoken disproportionately by well-to-do people. Second, you had access to resources enough to buy this book—either your own or those of another person, organization or church. (Wealthy once removed is still wealthy.)

Wealth, in and of itself, is nothing of which one should be ashamed; nor is poverty. Like poverty, wealth can be a challenge to faith. Having it can produce a sense of entitlement, of grandeur, and especially of sufficiency. When a check can be written to answer virtually any need or caprice, one can forget about the One who is behind it all. God provides wealth. God sustains wealth. We may make wise decisions that assist the processes, but ultimately we are in control of none of it. Trusting in our abilities and resources apart from God will inevitably put us in the position of the rich farmer in Luke 12—blessed beyond measure, only to die and have his riches pass on and enjoyed by another, wasted or lost.

The bigger issue with wealth is that it wholly ignores the greater issues of life. Material things, ever-present and ever-pressing before our eyes, are not all-important. In fact, the issues that remain invisible—our relationship with God foremost among them—have absolutely nothing to do with how many or how little material possessions one has. It makes no difference in the greater issues of life.

¹ Hear this, all you peoples;
  listen all who inhabit the world,
² both low and high,
  rich and poor together.
³ My mouth speaks wisdom;
  my heart's meditation brings
    understanding
⁴ I turn my ear to a proverb;
  I explain my riddle with a lyre.
⁵ Why should I fear in times of
    trouble?
  The iniquity of my foes surrounds
    me.
⁶ They trust in their wealth
  and boast of their abundant
    riches.
⁷ Yet these cannot redeem a person
  or pay his ransom to God—
⁸ since the price of redeeming him
    is too costly,
  one should forever stop trying—
⁹ so that he may live forever
  and not see the Pit.
¹⁰ For one can see that wise men
    die;
  the foolish and the senseless also
    pass away.
  Then they leave their wealth to
    others.
¹¹ Their graves are their eternal
    homes,
  their homes from generation to
    generation,

though they have named
   estates after themselves.
¹² But despite his assets, man will
      not last;
   he is like the animals that
      perish.
¹³ This is the way of those who are
      arrogant,
   and of their followers,
   who approve of their words.
                              Selah.
¹⁴ Like sheep they are headed for
      Sheol;
   Death will shepherd them.
   The upright will rule over them in
      the morning,
   and their form will waste away in
      Sheol,
   far from their lofty abode.
¹⁵ But God will redeem my life
   from the power of Sheol,
   for He will take me.   *Selah.*
¹⁶ Do not be afraid when a man
      gets rich,
   when the wealth of his house
      increases.
¹⁷ For when he dies, he will take
      nothing at all,
   his wealth will not follow him down.
¹⁸ Though he praises himself
      during his lifetime—
   and people praise you when you
      do well for yourself—
¹⁹ he will go to the generation of
      his fathers;
   they will never see the light.
²⁰ A man with valuable possessions
   but without understanding
   is like the animals that perish.

The sons of Korah encourage the people, most of whom were looking up from the lower classes at their rich oppressors with some envy and resentment, to stay faithful in their commitment to God. After all, God will be the judge of us all in due course of time. The special consideration we may feel the rich have acquired for themselves because of their status will avail them not at all in God's court.

Again, we are wealthy. Is it not the case that we can assume we are better off in God's eyes than we think we are? Do we assume, as Job's friends did, material blessings from God mean we are in good standing with Him? Or, perhaps more likely, do we simply cease to focus on eternal things since we take so much pleasure in temporary, earthly things?

Jesus says in Luke 9:24, "For whoever wants to save his life will lose it, but whoever loses his life because of Me will save it." The one universal constant about life on earth, regardless of how it is lived, is it will end. If you invest wholly here, you will lose everything. But if you consider life on earth, however completely or incompletely we may think ourselves blessed in it, to be simply an investment in eternity, we will find more life than we could imagine.

1. How do wealthy people threaten the people of God? How might we be a hazard to others because of our wealth? _____
_____
_____
_____

2. Is there a benefit in trying to extend one's life on earth? What are the benefits and dangers? _____
_____
_____
_____

> ### Figure of Speech
> **Sheol**
>
> Two words are used throughout the Old Testament, especially in the Psalms, to describe the state of the dead. The Holman Christian Standard Bible describes the word it translates Sheol as "A Hebrew word for either the grave or the realm of the dead." It similarly defines the word it renders "the Pit." Common people not wealthy enough for funerals would have been thrown into a common grave, little better than a hole. Psalm 49:9 indicates the wealthy will inevitably wind up in the same position as the poor in death, regardless of what provisions they may make for themselves.
>
> General discussion about the afterlife borrows not only from the Bible but from other sources. Specifically attaching "Sheol" to hell, heaven, Gehenna, Tartarus, Hades, or any other term, Biblical or not, misses the point. More often than not, Sheol is simply the alternative to life on earth—the destination of all the dead, whether a specific location, a spiritual realm, or merely a tomb.

3. What attitude should we have toward others who accumulate wealth? Is it appropriate to respond with fear or hatred? Explain. _____
_____
_____
_____

4. What is your favorite line in the psalm and why? _____
_____
_____
_____

The Wealthy: A Bible Study

Even Christians have trouble focusing on spiritual things in a carnal world. And prosperity makes it much more difficult. Such seems to have been the case for the church in Laodicea. The Laodicean church, as with many or most others, took upon itself the characteristics of its surroundings. For better or for worse, Laodicea was a very prosperous area.

Laodicea was well known for high-quality black wool. It is not known for a certainty today whether the cloth was because of the sheep themselves, which may have produced an unusually fine fleece, or whether the cloth was dyed. In any case, Laodicean black wool and garments made from it were in high demand.

Additionally, one of the most acclaimed medical schools in the world was in Laodicea. Most notably, a salve had been developed there to treat a variety of eye ailments. People from all over the world would come to Laodicea for healing.

Because of the remarkable wealth developed in these industries, a banking industry developed generating its own revenue. History says the city was brought to the ground by an earthquake in the First Century but refused funds from Rome to rebuild, choosing instead to finance the reconstruction locally.

For all its prosperity, Laodicea lacked one essential resource: water. Cold springs were in abundance in nearby Colossae, and hot springs near Hierapolis. Both arrived in Laodicea at a lukewarm temperature, unfit for most purposes other than irrigation.

Jesus makes use of all of these considerations when lecturing the church in Revelation 3:14-22. The church, like the city, had grown self-sufficient (in its own eyes) because of the economic prosperity it enjoyed. The individual members, it seems, were also wealthy—at least, more so than most of their contemporaries. But they had turned lukewarm about spiritual things. The opportunity to revel in the flesh had taken their eyes off of heaven and the Lord.

The things they valued in their community were worthless compared to the spiritual blessings Jesus was trying to provide. He says in verse 18, "I advise you to buy from me gold refined in the fire so that you may be rich, and white clothes so that you may be dressed and your shameful nakedness not be exposed, and ointment to spread on your eyes so that you may see."

Read Psalm 49 again—this time with the Laodiceans in mind.

1. What would be a warning sign that we are too "rich" for our own good? Do we see that sign? _____
   _____
   _____
   _____

2. How would a "hot" or "cold" Christian look? How might a "lukewarm" Christian be worse than either? _____
   _____
   _____
   _____

Psalm 73—A Parallel Study

"I envied the arrogant; I saw the prosperity of the wicked." Psalm 73:3 sums up the problem we often have with money. It's not that we have so little; it's other people—people we deem unworthy—who have so much. We are embarrassed to think they have chosen a better way than the Lord's way. But we can't help thinking it from time to time.

As verse 17 indicates, worship changes our thinking. Focusing on God instead of our problems (or others' successes) brings us back to God's reality. It is "a fool…an unreasoning animal" (v.22) who thinks life is all about being comfortable in the short term.

1. Why does God not make blessings in this life parallel to one's spiritual status?
___
___
___
___

2. How is speaking aloud of our doubts a betrayal of the people of God (v.15)? Is it ever appropriate to share spiritual weaknesses with brethren? ___
___
___
___

3. What does God do for us that, as verse 28 indicates, we should tell people? Are the people of the world interested in such things? ___
___
___
___

4. What is your favorite line in the psalm and why? ___
___
___
___

The Wealthy: A Case Study

Liam was going to be a big success. Everyone knew it, even before he went to college. His parents knew, his peers knew, certainly Liam knew. He did not disappoint anyone. He quickly acquired a degree in finance, an MBA, and was riding the crest of the bull market to a lucrative career as a financial advisor. He was quick to offer his services to the brethren, but he refused to profit from them, insisting on donating all his commissions to the church along with his already sizeable contributions.

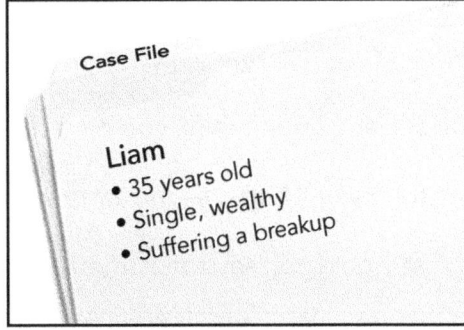

Case File

Liam
- 35 years old
- Single, wealthy
- Suffering a breakup

It's not that Liam was obnoxious or egotistical about his wealth; it was more that he seemed at times incapable of talking about anything else. News discussions turned toward the stock market; sports discussions turned toward salary structures; vacation planning turned toward revenue streams. It seemed like the pursuit of money completely consumed him.

When his girlfriend, Jill, broke up with him, Liam's world was shaken for the first time in his adult life. They had been dating for four years; Liam had delayed proposing marriage until he was sure she loved him and not just his money. Ironically, he had already bought a four-carat diamond ring and planned an elaborate presentation ceremony to take place over the Christmas holiday; she ended it with him three weeks before that.

"I know you got tired of waiting," Liam said to her, desperate. "I'm sorry. I waited way too long. But I'm ready. I've been ready for months. I wanted to make this extra special for you, but we don't have to do that. We can get married today, be on a plane for Paris tonight, spend a month touring Europe. It will be the honeymoon of your dreams."

"See, that's what the problem is," Jill said, tearing up. "Everything is about money and what it will buy with you. But I'm not something you can buy, Liam."

"I know! I would never try to do that!"

"But you're doing it now! The truth is, you don't know what I want. I've never once told you I wanted to go to Paris. Not once."

"I'm sorry. Really. Tell me where you do want to go."

"I've told you a hundred times, Liam. And the fact that you don't know where that place is proves what I'm saying. I'll take your ring right now if you can take me where I've always dreamed of going."

Liam's face lit up with excitement, then darkened with panic as he racked his brain, trying to remember. "Uh, … uh …"

"Heaven, Liam. I want to go to heaven."

"Oh, of course! I know that!"

"No, Liam, I don't think you do."

Read Psalm 49 again—this time with Liam in mind.

What would you say to Liam, based on Psalm 49? _____
_____
_____
_____

New Testament Insight

*Yet these cannot redeem a person
or pay his ransom to God—
since the price of redeeming him is too costly,
one should forever stop trying—
so that he may live forever
and not see the Pit.* — Psalm 49:7-9

Wealth brings a sense of self-sufficiency concerning the problems and potential problems coming up in this world. "How much will it cost to make the problem go away?" There is always a number.

The "problem" we have in the spiritual world is far bigger than that. Money cannot redeem the sinner. There is no number.

Ephesians 2:1-10 likens our situation to being dead. Dead people have no say in the matter of being dead or not dead. No price can be paid—not by us. Suggesting there is, that we can do something on our end to earn us a home in glory, is a philosophy often called "salvation by works." The Bible expressly excludes it. Achieving a right relationship with God by our resources, abilities and skills would elevate us as being worthy instead of elevating our Savior, who is truly worthy.

Salvation by grace does little for our egos. It does not make us better than anyone else; quite the opposite, in fact. We are not worth saving; none of us is. Thanks be to God; we don't have to be.

The Wealthy: A Hymn Study

It was late one night in 1934 in Springfield, Missouri, and Lloyd Otis Sanderson could not sleep. A piece of music was stuck in his head, waiting to be written, and he could not rest until he put it on paper. But it was an unusual meter, one that didn't fit any hymn lyrics he knew. So he wrote to Thomas Obediah Chisholm, a frequent collaborator ("A New Creature," "Bring Christ Your Broken Life"), and asked him to contribute some words to go along with his composition. Little did he realize that Chisholm, miles away in New Jersey, had been unable to sleep on that same night and had composed hymn lyrics that were awaiting appropriate music. Sanderson's tune and Chisolm's lyric combined perfectly to form "Be With Me, Lord," a hymn beloved and regularly used ever since.

Leon B. Sanderson, son of L.O., considers "Be With Me, Lord" to be perhaps the best loved of his father's many hymns. As he points out, hymns equally appropriate at weddings and funerals are hard to find. Often the lyrics are tweaked a bit to fit the occasion—"Be with us, Lord" for group meetings, "Be with them, Lord" for weddings, etc.

Chisolm published 800 hymns in total including "Great is Thy Faithfulness," "O to be Like Thee!," "Only in Thee" and "Living for Jesus." Although most noted for his compositions, Sanderson also occasionally wrote lyrics—including "Where Livest Thou?" and "Pray All the Time"—using the pseudonym Vana R. Raye. He also wrote the hymn given to the title of his autobiography, *The Lord Has Been Mindful of Me*.

The Wealthy: A Worship Study

"So, is everyone wondering why I picked 'Be With Me, Lord,' as a song to focus on in a lesson on wealth?"

Lisa's hand shot up, as was often the case with the precocious 10-year-old. "Because you couldn't find a good song about money?"

"That's not too far wrong," I said through the laughter. "They don't write a lot of hymns about getting rich, do they? But I had to come up with something. And I kept coming back to Psalm 49:20—'A man with valuable possessions but without understanding is like the animals that perish.' And I thought if we can't sing about spending our money properly, maybe we can sing about how it's not our money that makes us rich. It's our relationship with God, right?"

"It's a lot better to have God with you than to have a lot of money," Lisa pointed out.

"Why is that?"

"Well, there are a lot of dangers and problems that would cost more money to fix than you would have. But if you have God, it doesn't matter how bad the problems are. He is strong enough for anything."

"Good point, Lisa. It's like it says in the third verse—'a constant sense of Thy abiding presence.' I don't know if that's the best present God could give us, or if Mr. Chisholm was suggesting it was. But there's certainly nothing like it—no doubt about it."

What does "Be With Me, Lord" mean to you? _____
_____
_____
_____

The Bible Study Song List

If you were putting a list together for a study about wealth, what songs would you include and why? _____
_____
_____

What songs might you exclude and why? _____
_____
_____

Psalm 50
A Song for the Hypocrite

In many ways, we live in a very religious culture. Most Americans consider themselves believers in God. Most are at least somewhat interested in spiritual things. Public figures pronounce their devotion to Jesus Christ on a regular basis. We are told repeatedly that we are, or were, a "Christian nation"—by those who wish it to be so, and by those who do not. The emphasis on basic Biblical morality is so ingrained in our society (from the posting of the Ten Commandments at local courthouses to references to God in our founding documents) that we may think it reasonable to expect righteous behavior from our neighbors. And sometimes we do expect it.

Unfortunately, many people are far better at voicing their trust in God than they are at practicing it. They befriend the wicked, blaspheme the righteous, and completely ignore God's word concerning day-to-day living. Despite our urge, like James and John, to ask the Lord to summon immediate justice from the heavens (Luke 9:54), God remains strangely silent.

The hypocrite sees God's inaction and is emboldened. "You have done these things, and I kept silent; you thought I was just like you," (v.21). After all, they would never tolerate such a display of disrespect. They would never suffer indignity when they had the option of avoiding it. They would never allow a slight to go unchallenged or a crime to go unpunished. So why would God? But again, God is not like us (thankfully). He does not feel compelled to show His hand immediately. Sometimes in His wisdom, He

¹ God, the LORD God speaks;
He summons the earth from east to west.
² From Zion, the perfection of beauty,
God appears in radiance.
³ Our God is coming; He will not be silent!
Devouring fire precedes Him,
and a storm rages around Him.
⁴ On high, He summons heaven and earth
in order to judge His people.
⁵ "Gather My faithful ones to Me,
those who make a covenant with Me by sacrifice."
⁶ The heavens proclaim His righteousness,
for God is the judge.   *Selah.*
⁷ "Listen, My people, and I will speak;
I will testify against you, Israel.
I am God, your God.
⁸ I do not rebuke you for your sacrifices
or for your burnt offerings,
which are continually before Me.
⁹ I will not accept a bull from your household
or male goats from your pens,
¹⁰ for every animal of the forest is Mine,
the cattle on a thousand hills.
¹¹ I know every bird of the mountains,
and the creatures of the field are Mine.

¹² If I were hungry, I would not tell you,
for the world and everything in it is Mine.
¹³ Do I eat the flesh of bulls
or drink the blood of goats?
¹⁴ Sacrifice a thank offering to God,
and pay your vows to the Most High.
¹⁵ Call on Me in a day of trouble;
I will rescue you, and you will honor Me."
¹⁶ But God says to the wicked:
"What right do you have to recite My statutes
and to take My covenant on your lips?
¹⁷ You hate instruction,
and turn your back on My words.
¹⁸ When you see a thief,
you make friends with him,
and you associate with adulterers.
¹⁹ You unleash your mouth for evil
and harness your tongue for deceit.
²⁰ You sit, maligning your brother,
slandering your mother's son.
²¹ You have done these things, and I kept silent;
you thought I was just like you.
But I will rebuke you
and lay out the case before you.
²² "Understand this, you who forget God,
or I will tear you apart,
and there will be no rescuer.
²³ Whoever sacrifices a thank offering honors Me,
and whoever orders his conduct,
I will show him the salvation of God."

decides to wait. So we, still frustrated, muster our faith and wait with Him.

Perhaps the worst hypocrisy is when people use a shallow understanding of Scripture to rationalize behavior that is opposed to God's clear, unambiguous and frequently repeated plan for our lives. Such "students" of the Word are only honoring their wisdom; God's wisdom will have little impact on them, and they will have little impact in the world for God.

The hypocrisy of pseudo-Christians shows up during worship as it does before and after. God says in verse 8 that He did not rebuke them for their continual offerings; yet in verse 9 He says He will not accept them. Why not? The context supports the idea that He is rejecting their attitude more than their activity. God does not want another animal; He has them all already. He wants our hearts. If we give Him that, along with our worship, we can call on Him with every hope that He will be there for us.

1. According to verses 1-6, is it a terrifying thing or a glorious thing to see God coming in judgment against His people? Explain. _____
_____
_____
_____
_____
_____

2. What are some examples of Scriptures "taken out of context" to prove an unscriptural point? Cite Scripture to show God's attitude to such usage of His word.
_____
_____
_____
_____
_____
_____

> ### A Thousand Hills
> **Figure of Speech**
>
> Exactly how many hills there are in the world depends somewhat on how one defines a hill. It is reasonable to assume there are far more than a thousand. Trying to count exactly how many cattle are on the thousand we may isolate is a colossal waste of effort. The exact number is not important. The message is, God already owns far more than we could ever hope to give back to Him.
>
> Powers of ten are used countless times (millions of times a day, we might say) to demonstrate vastness of scope. One example is in 2 Peter 3:8, "with the Lord one day is like 1,000 years, and 1,000 years like one day." Throughout Revelation are found numbers with multiple zeros always depicting immense hordes; Revelation 5:11, 9:16 and 14:1 are a few examples. Sometimes in the text such numbers are given to give a rough idea of real numbers (1 Kings 8:63, 11:3); often, though, the idea is less specific. Context will help the reader determine how literally to take the wording.

3. What are some ways God's people today can find themselves making friends with thieves, associate with adulterers, etc.? Is this always a good thing or a bad thing? _____
   _____
   _____
   _____

4. What is your favorite line in the psalm and why? _____
   _____
   _____
   _____

The Hypocrite: A Bible Study

There's something suspicious about that story.

She's an adulteress. OK, it happens. Sad, but true. She got caught. Again, it happens. Not always, but sometimes. But this one was "caught in the act of committing adultery" (John 8:4). In the act. That's rare, especially in the days before hidden microphones and drone cameras.

Where is the man? If she was "caught in the act," surely he was as well. Are we to believe he was just faster or more elusive than she? Did he make a move like Joseph and leave his garment in his would-be captors' hands?

Perhaps, just perhaps, catching both consenting parties wasn't ever the plan.

Would it be unreasonable to suggest that the scribes and Pharisees staged the entire episode just to put Jesus in an untenable situation? Remember, these are the very men who rationalized the abandonment of one's parents (Matthew 15:3-6), who suborned perjury at the capital trial of a man they knew to be innocent (Matthew 26:59-60), and who no doubt in many other ways well earned Jesus' abject scorn; "Snakes! Brood of vipers!" He called them (Matthew 23:33). Isn't it, at least, conceivable that the entire episode in John 8:2-11 was a put-up job?

It certainly would fit the way Jesus responded to them. In other situations in which He was asked to respond to controversial statements or situations, He had an uncanny ability to cut through the balderdash and hone in on the central issue at hand, whether it was the shallow faith of the Sadducees (Matthew 22:23-32) or the Pharisees' unwillingness to elevate the Messiah over the great king David (Matthew 22:41-46). The woman caught in adultery was sinful, no doubt; we all are. But the self-righteous accusers were every bit as much given over to the devil as she was.

So instead of agreeing to sentence her to death (which no doubt would have brought on the wrath of the Romans) or commuting her sentence (which would have shown disrespect to the Law of Moses in front of His disciples), He ignored them. Finally, He made one simple statement, defusing the entire situation—"The one without sin among you should be the first to throw a stone at her" (John 8:7). Surely He did not mean one would need to be completely sinless to accuse someone of a crime; the Law of Moses is replete with admonitions to give witness to crimes. No, He means here being "without sin" in the current situation; one who is less guilty than the woman should make the accusation. Of course, no one could.

Not being a witness to the crime prevented Jesus from testifying; that is why He refused to condemn her particular action. He maintained His commitment to obedience that He enjoined on others (Matthew 5:19-20), and so told her, "Neither do I condemn you…from now on do not sin any more" (John 8:11). Jesus was no hypocrite; He had condemned adultery to an extent that even the Pharisees did not (Matthew 5:27-28), and He condemned it still. However, He was just as opposed to other, less public, forms of sin. Knowing the sin in the hearts of all men (John 2:25), He condemned it all equally.

Read Psalm 50 again—this time with the woman caught in adultery in mind.

1. Do we have a different attitude toward different kinds of sin? Should we? __
   _____
   _____
   _____

2. How does love for our sinful neighbors (and brethren) fit in with our need to expose sin? _____
   _____
   _____
   _____

Psalm 15—A Parallel Study

The question of verse 1—"LORD, who can dwell in Your tent?"—presupposes a truth much of the religious world would deny: some people are not permitted entrance into the presence of God. David does not exclude ax murderers and rapists alone; the traits he includes cover basic, fundamental characteristics upheld throughout Scripture. And the first one is perhaps the most basic: "The one who lives honestly, practices righteousness, and acknowledges the truth in his heart" (v.2).

Think about it. If we have an iffy relationship with the truth in general, how is God to receive our praise and repentance? Even mere mortals who do not know perfectly "the ideas and thoughts of the heart" (Hebrews 4:12) know enough to reject the words of someone known for lying. Do we not think God Almighty can do the same?

Merely professing our faith—or saying, "Lord, Lord!" as Jesus puts it in Matthew 7:21—is not enough. We must back up our righteous talk with a righteous walk.

1. In your opinion, which of these characteristics are the most difficult to achieve for the people of God today? _____
   _____
   _____
   _____

2. In what sense do we despise those whom God rejects (v.4)? Is this compatible with loving our neighbor? _____
   _____
   _____
   _____

3. Is it appropriate for Christians to lend money? Is a modest interest rate and/or a written contract appropriate? _____
_____
_____
_____

4. What is your favorite line in the psalm and why? _____
_____
_____
_____

The Hypocrite: A Case Study

Case File

Paula
- 24 years old
- Single
- Caught engaging in "social dringkng"

Paula had no idea that Janine was dating a man in her office. If she had, she wouldn't have been drinking freely from the open bar at the Christmas party.

Janine, an elder's daughter and a frequent teacher at the monthly ladies' Bible study, was shocked and aghast. Paula, herself a deacon's wife and frequent teacher, had been sitting with Janine at lunch just a few weeks earlier when a discussion of social drinking had taken place. Janine had been firmly against it; so, she thought, had Paula.

"I know what you're thinking," Paula said after Janine pulled her aside to talk. "But this is not what it looks like."

"It looks like you're drinking a glass of wine!"

"It's my first," Paula insisted. "And my last. I have a glass once in a while at these things, just to fit in."

"It doesn't smell like your first," Janine said, waving her hand in front of her face to clear the fumes.

"Janine! Honest, I wouldn't lie to you!"

"You've told me numerous times you didn't drink. Weren't those lies?"

"Look, it's no big deal. I'll not drink anymore, OK? No harm done."

"Don't you understand? I only agreed to come here tonight with Mitch if he promised he would not drink. We were only going to stop by for a half-hour or so and then leave. But he's seen you. And he knows we are members of the same church. How am I supposed to explain this to him? I'm trying to convince him that Christians can say no to this sort of thing, and here you are half-baked!"

"Well, I didn't know you two were dating."

"What difference does that make? You should be setting an example for him yourself."

"And I am, I am," Paula said, leaning in to put a hand on Janine's shoulder. "Look, I'm not 'half-baked.' I'm fine. I'm sorry if I upset you. Let's just let it go, OK?"

"What do you mean, 'let it go'?"

Paula leaned in and whispered, "I mean, you're not going to tell your father, are you?"

Janine pushed back, repulsed by the smell on Paula's breath. "What do you care if I tell him? It doesn't sound to me like you think you are doing anything wrong."

"Well, I'm not sure I am. But I don't want any trouble with the elders. It's not anyone's business what I do in my private time."

"I think you and I have very different ideas about what 'private time' means," Janine said, turning to leave. "And about a lot of other things, too, it looks like."

Read Psalm 50 again — this time with Paula in mind.

What would you say to Paula based on Psalm 50? _____
_____
_____
_____

New Testament Insight

*I know every bird of the mountains,
and the creatures of the field are Mine.* — Psalm 50:11

God's point in Psalm 50:11 is that mankind need not worry that He will have to go hungry if His people do not cook enough animals on His altar for Him. He knows all of His creation, including the animal kingdom. As He mentions in verse 12, even if He did get hungry (and we have no indication God does), He would be far more able to supply His need than we would be able to supply it for Him.

God's interaction with the creation indicates more than mere knowledge. His awareness of the most minute aspect of the world surrounding us emboldens us to think we are known just as intimately. Our needs, our problems, our doubts, our fears—our God knows it all.

In Luke 12:24, Jesus turns the consideration of ministering to God's "needs" to His willingness to minister to ours—"Consider the ravens: they don't sow or reap; they don't have a storeroom or a barn; yet God feeds them. Aren't you worth much more than the birds?" If God can care for the birds, that assures us of His concern for us. "Aren't two sparrows sold for a penny? Yet not one of them falls to the ground without your Father's consent. But even the hairs of your head have all been counted. Don't be afraid therefore; you are worth more than many sparrows" (Matthew 10:29-31).

The Hypocrite: A Hymn Study

Oswald Smith was 21 in 1911. He had been invited to speak at the largest Methodist church in Woodstock, Ontario. While walking to the assembly hall, a melody popped into his mind along with the simple lyric, "Into the heart of Jesus, deeper and deeper I go." He managed to retain it in his memory long enough to get it written down. The music was finished almost immediately; the full lyric took three years to complete. At the end of it, the young man, who had since entered full-time preaching work, had a hymn that would delight worshipers for decades.

The theme of the hymn—moving from a shallow understanding of the fundamental things of Jesus to a deeper, more fulfilling relationship based on a real, deep-seated commitment—is reflected somewhat in Smith's life. Beginning at age 13, when a Bible class teacher suggested that one of the students there might one day be a minister, he found himself as a young man growing more and more involved in church work. Stymied by his attempts to begin mission work at the age of 18, he took it upon himself to find opportunities to preach, including in impoverished areas among Indian tribes.

Various preaching positions eventually led him to Toronto, where he founded what became The People's Church, the largest church in Canada. He raised an estimated $14 million to support preaching in remote destinations, half of which came from his congregation. His preaching travels took him to 72 countries, and his radio ministry reached untold numbers.

From "Deeper and Deeper," Smith went on to write more than 1,200 hymns, none of which are in common usage among churches of Christ. Smith preached his final sermon at the age of 92 at People's Church and died January 25, 1986. George Beverly Shea sang at his funeral, and Billy Graham preached.

Psalm 50—A Song for the Hypocrite | 81

Deeper and Deeper

1. In-to the heart of Jesus, Deep-er and deep-er I go,
Seek-ing to know the rea-son Why He should love me so,
Why He should stoop to lift me Up from the mir-y clay,
Sav-ing my soul, mak-ing me whole, Though I had wan-dered a-way.

2. In-to the will of Jesus, Deep-er and deep-er I go,
Pray-ing for grace to fol-low, Seek-ing His way to know,
Bow-ing in full sur-ren-der Low at His bless-ed feet,
Bid-ding Him take, break me and make, Till I am mold-ed, com-plete.

3. In-to the cross of Jesus, Deep-er and deep-er I go,
Fol-low-ing through the gar-den, Fac-ing the dread-ed foe;
Drink-ing the cup of sor-row, Sob-bing with bro-ken heart:
O Sav-ior, help! Dear Sav-ior, help! Grace for my weak-ness im-part."

4. In-to the joy of Jesus, Deep-er and deep-er I go,
Ris-ing, with soul en-rap-tured Far from the world be-low;
Joy in the place of sor-row, Peace in the midst of pain,
Je-sus will give, Je-sus will give; He will up-hold and sus-tain.

Words: Oswald J. Smith
Music: Oswald J. Smith

The Hypocrite: A Worship Study

Hypocrisy hymns featured in our hymnals are few and far between. We took the occasion to emphasize the flipside to hypocrisy—unfeigned, unapologetic, consistent devotion to Christ knowing no boundaries and submitting to no schedule. "Deeper and Deeper" featured prominently.

"So what do songs like 'Deeper and Deeper' teach us about hypocrisy?" I asked.

"I think it's about our intentions," said Pete. "So many people out there—and plenty in the church, I guess—are just interested in looking like Christians. To other people, I mean. If they keep their sins to themselves, if no one finds out about it, well, that may not be exactly hunky-dory, but it 's not as bad as it might be. And they think they can live with that. They do live with that."

"Surely there's nothing wrong with looking like a Christian," I said.

"But that shouldn't be our motivation. Trying to do what people want us to do will keep us from being slaves of Christ. Paul says that in Galatians 1:10. And in Ephesians, he says children of light are supposed to be always learning what pleases God, not men."

"Ephesians 5:10, right," I added. "And if looking religious were our motivation, we would run the serious risk of doing what the majority of people in our society think a Christian would or should do, versus what God says he should do. And those two things aren't nearly as similar as they should be, given the degree of false doctrine and Biblical compromise that's out there these days."

"But if we focus on going 'deeper and deeper' into our relationship with Jesus, we might be less inclined to dwell on others' expectations. And when those expectations are not in harmony with Jesus' expectations, we are that much more inclined to choose the right path."

What does "Deeper and Deeper" mean to you? _____
_____
_____

The Bible Study Song List

If you were putting a list together for a study about hypocrisy, what songs would you include and why? _____
_____
_____

What songs might you exclude and why? _____
_____
_____

Psalm 51
A Song for the Guilty

Christians love grace. We believe God will forgive us of our sins, regardless of what they are or how many of them there may be. But there comes a time in the lives of most if not all Christians when we, rightly or wrongly, feel the need to beg. And beg we do.

Even though our sins frequently affect others for ill, we apologize to God first. Sin is, at its core, an offense against God. "Against You—You alone—I have sinned," David says in Psalm 51:4. That is the problem with repentance often; we convince ourselves our crime is victimless and, therefore, inconsequential. The sinner is the ultimate and greatest victim of sin. It costs him his relationship with God—which is to say, it costs him everything.

Those who have a relationship with the heavenly Father can have confidence their guilt, though horrific, need not be permanent. Verse 1 says it all: Our God is gracious; our God is loving; our God is compassionate. Just as our earthly fathers are willing to bear with our weaknesses and failures, so also our heavenly Father bears with us.

The guilt we bear is the guilt of our sins; the psalm makes that clear. David requests forgiveness for "my sin" and "my rebellion" (v.2-3). "My guilt" is directly attached to "my sins" (v.9). It is what is deep within us that has gone awry, not some transgression committed by someone else—parents, Adam, society, or anyone else. The sin on our record is our violation of God's moral and legal code. Therefore, the remedy is

¹ Be gracious to me, God,
  according to Your faithful love;
  according to Your abundant
    compassion,
  blot out my rebellion.
² Wash away my guilt,
  and cleanse me from my sin.
³ For I am conscious of my
    rebellion,"
  and my sin is always before me.
⁴ Against You—You alone—I have
    sinned
  and done this evil in Your sight.
  So You are right when You pass
    sentence;
  You are blameless when You
    judge.
⁵ Indeed, I was guilty when I was
    born;
  I was sinful when my mother
    conceived me.
⁶ Surely You desire integrity in the
    inner self,
  and You teach me wisdom deep
    within.
⁷ Purify me with hyssop, and I will
    be clean;
  wash me, and I will be whiter
    than snow.
⁸ Let me hear joy and gladness;
  let the bones You have crushed
    rejoice.
⁹ Turn Your face away from my sins
  and blot out all my guilt.

¹⁰ God, create a clean heart for me
and renew a steadfast spirit within me.
¹¹ Do not banish me from Your presence
or take Your Holy Spirit from me.
¹² Restore the joy of Your salvation to me,
and give me a willing spirit.
¹³ Then I will teach the rebellious Your ways,
and sinners will return to You.
¹⁴ Save me from the guilt of bloodshed, God,
the God of my salvation,
and my tongue will sing of Your righteousness.
¹⁵ Lord, open my lips,
and my mouth will declare Your praise.
¹⁶ You do not want a sacrifice, or I would give it;
You are not pleased with a burnt offering.
¹⁷ The sacrifice pleasing to God is a broken spirit.
God, You will not despise a broken and humbled heart.
¹⁸ In Your good pleasure cause Zion to prosper;
build the walls of Jerusalem.
¹⁹ Then You will delight in righteous sacrifices,
whole burnt offerings;
then bulls will be offered on Your altar.

directed toward ourselves: "Surely You desire integrity in the inner self, and You teach me wisdom deep within. Purify me with hyssop, and I will be clean; wash me, and I will be whiter than snow" (v.6-7).

Secondary consequences of our sin and guilt are touched on by David at the conclusion of the psalm; verse 18 indicates the prosperity of the people of God, in general, has suffered because of David's sin. Certainly this is in part because David was the king, and frequently in Israel's history the nation suffered because of the king's sin. There is a very real sense in which our failings impact the whole spiritual body. The health of the whole depends on "the proper working of each individual part" (Ephesians 4:16). If we can address the transgression in our lives properly, we can be in a better position not only to serve God ourselves but also to assist our brethren in doing so.

1. What is hyssop? Explain its significance in verse 7. _____
_____
_____
_____
_____
_____

2. In what sense does God "create a clean heart for me" (v.10)? Do we have personal responsibility to make a clean heart for ourselves, or does God do all the work?
_____
_____
_____
_____
_____
_____

> ### Figure of Speech
>
> **Guilty When I Was Born**
>
> Those familiar with the language of the Psalms will not be surprised to see examples of hyperbole. It is impossible to conceive of God holding babies accountable for sin, even at the very point of conception (v.5). Jesus says we are to be "converted and become like children" (Matthew 18:3)—an image rendered pointless if children need to be converted.
>
> Sin is an individual choice as described throughout the text (James 4:17, 1 John 3:4). "Rebellion" (v.3) requires consciousness of sin. The context of Psalm 51 describes David's sins as a grown man, particularly his sins concerning Uriah and Bathsheba.
>
> Flawed, weak humans waste little time in getting into sin. That is even true for a man who is habitually "loyal to Him" like David (1 Samuel 13:14). Thankfully we, like David, are received back into fellowship, cleansed from sin, when we repent and turn back to Him.

3. Explain verse 16 in the context of the Law of Moses. Did God really not care whether the people offered the prescribed sacrifices for sin? _____
_____
_____
_____

4. What is your favorite line in the psalm and why? _____
_____
_____
_____

The Guilty: A Bible Study

There is something cathartic about getting caught in sin when you are a child of God. You know in your heart of hearts what you are doing is wrong. You fully expect to stop eventually, but you can't seem to muster up the energy. Then, suddenly, you are forced to stop. The lies are exposed. The lingering feeling of dread is gone. You are compelled to do what you know you must do, the only thing you can do. After having done so, you feel immensely better—even if the consequences of getting caught are extreme.

David's attitude regarding the exposure of his sin with Uriah and Bathsheba in 2 Samuel 12 is a great example. Surely "a man after God's own heart," as we often say, paraphrasing 1 Samuel 13:14, knew what he was doing was sinful long before Nathan the prophet labeled it as such. He was outraged at the similar behavior committed by the fictional rich man in Nathan's parable. We have to believe he was outraged at his own. Still, it seems he was willing to sweep things under the rug and keep them there as long as possible, somehow convincing himself that avoiding public notoriety was the same thing as avoiding God's judgment.

When he realized his sin was not private, and the man of God (presumably others as well) knew about it, a sense of resignation and perhaps even relief came over him. "I have sinned against the LORD," he says simply in 2 Samuel 12:13. As simple as his expression of repentance is, so is Nathan's reply in the next verse: "The LORD has taken away your sin; you will not die."

Perhaps we may feel in our moment of secret sin that being exposed to our family, the church and the world is a fate worse than death. In fact, the reverse is true. By continuing to cover up the sin, we compound it. We continue to wrong those who are close to us. We continue to rebel against God's will for our lives. Sin brings death, not embarrassment. The consequences of dealing with confession's aftermath may be extreme, but it is highly unlikely to be as extreme as those given to David—the loss of his newborn son. There are no consequences for sin in this life that could compare to what happens when we refuse to confess sin. Once we realized this, we are likely to respond to our consequences much as David did: pray that they are mitigated, regret it deeply if they are not, and, in any case, pick ourselves up at the end of it and continue, grateful for a second chance at life.

Read Psalm 51 again—this time with David in mind.

1. How can "a man after God's own heart" drift so far into sin? How can it be avoided? How can it be stopped once it starts? _____
_____
_____
_____

2. What would be a different, less noble way to respond to someone who points out your sin? What would cause a person to react this way? _____
_____
_____
_____

Psalm 38—A Parallel Study

Guilt often produces physical symptoms in the bodies of the guilty. Ulcers, stress headaches, and worse are not uncommon. Beyond these, there are psychological problems. Sullenness, outbursts of anger, isolation, and other issues regularly make life even worse for the guilty soul.

Psalm 38 describes both categories of pain in the life of the sinner. The loss of fellowship with God is compounded by the loss of health, worsening personal relationships, and increasing despair in the face of opposition.

1. Is suffering in the flesh necessarily a sign of sin? If not, how do we know when and if it is? _____
_____
_____

2. Are consequences of sin automatically reversed upon confession? If not, what is the motivation to confess? _____
_____
_____

3. Is it a good thing or a bad thing that God knows our "every desire" (v.9)? Explain. _____
_____
_____

4. What is your favorite line in the psalm and why? _____
_____
_____

The Guilty: A Case Study

When the elders announced Dean was going to be accepted back into fellowship, the reaction was, at best, mixed. Dean, after all, had been directly responsible for the darkest time in the history of the congregation. After preaching there for five years, it was discovered he engaged in a sexual relationship with a woman in the church—the wife of one of the deacons—for most of it. Finally, the woman gave the elders a letter to be read in front of the congregation, confessing her sin. Dean left the building in the middle of the reading; his wife and children had to find other ways home that night. In what seemed at the time to be a mere instant, Dean had resigned, both

Case File

Dean
- 36 years old
- Divorced, former preacher
- Coming back to the church he hurt

marriages were over, several families had left the church, and one elder—Dean's closest friend—had stepped down.

Three months later, after attending sporadically at various area churches (all of which were, at least, an hour from his house), Dean was back. Although his wife and children had relocated, he had managed to keep his house and find a job locally. He wanted forgiveness, and he wanted acceptance back into fellowship.

"There is no question of him being hired again as our local preacher," the elder said to the congregation. "In fact, we have decided—and Dean agrees with our decision—not to have him in the pulpit at all during the process of finding a full-time evangelist. Whether we are going to allow him to give a Wednesday night invitation six months down the road, well, we will decide that in six months.

"We are aware that having him here is going to be a reminder of a dark time from our recent past. It may be that some of you are thinking right now that you are going to be incapable of worshiping with Dean in the room. Ultimately, you will have to abide by the dictates of your conscience. Your elders have been praying and fasting over this issue for several days now, and we feel Dean genuinely wants to make things right with us, and he has already done so with God. God will be the judge of his heart, of course. If we believe God has forgiven him, we can see no justification for not forgiving him ourselves. And forgiving is about moving ahead to the future, not dwelling on the past.

"We urge you, brethren, to forgive. This challenging and, as you may imagine, impossible task we lay before you today is an opportunity. We can hold a grudge, allow the specter of guilt to linger indefinitely, and keep the gossip fires burning in the background. Or we can love a brother in the way God loves us, forgive a brother in the way God forgives us and get back the task of helping one another on the road to heaven."

Read Psalm 51 again—this time with Dean in mind.

What would you say to Dean based on Psalm 51? _____
_____
_____
_____

New Testament Insight

> *Wash away my guilt,*
> *and cleanse me from my sin.* — Psalm 51:2

The image of washing in connection with the removal of sins is common. It first occurs in Exodus 19:10, where the people of Israel were required to wash their clothes before their encounter with God at Mount Sinai. The law revealed there includes extensive cleansing processes, particularly for priests whose job it was to attend before the Lord in His house. The connection between physical filth and spiritual defilement is an easy one to make.

Christians are regularly presented either as having been washed or needing to be continually washed. In 1 Corinthians 6:11 it is said of saints that they had been "washed" from their previous sinful practices.

Some say passages such as Titus 3:5 and Ephesians 5:26 refer to Old Testament "washings" and not baptism—that "the washing of regeneration and renewal by the Holy Spirit" has nothing to do with immersion in water. But the "ritual washings" of Hebrew 6:2 are part of a context wholly composed of New Testament doctrines—indeed, fundamental doctrines that must be firmly established before the Christian moves on to maturity. We "wash away" sins by calling on Jesus' name in baptism, according to Acts 22:16. Even if the occasional "washing" passage isn't specifically about baptism, the doctrine of baptism for remission of sins (with or without reference to "washing") cannot be escaped (Acts 2:38, Romans 6:3-4, Galatians 3:27, 1 Peter 3:21, etc.).

The Guilty: A Hymn Study

Dr. James Edwin Orr was a prominent minister and author during much of the 20th Century. Born in 1912 in Belfast, Northern Ireland, Orr eventually made his base of operations in the United States, from which he ventured out to preach in 150 countries. He became one of the founding board members of Campus Crusade for Christ. Billy Graham called him "one of the greatest authorities on the history of religious revivals in the Protestant world."

In 1936, Orr was traveling in Ngaruawahia, New Zealand, and first became acquainted with the Maori Song of Farewell, "Po Ata Rau" (translated, "Now is the Hour"). Entranced by the melody, he could not get it out of his head. Shortly thereafter, he wrote a spiritual lyric to go along with it on the back of an envelope while waiting in the Ngaruawahia post office. Orr drew inspiration from Psalm 51:2 and Psalm 139:23-24. These lyrics became the hymn "Cleanse Me," also known as "Search Me, O God." The words of the third verse neatly encapsulate Orr's lifelong emphasis on energizing the church in spiritual activity: "Send a revival, start the work with me."

"Cleanse Me" was first published in one of Orr's books, *All You Need*. It has been recorded multiple times, including by Bill and Gloria Gaither. Orr wrote several other hymns, but none nearly so popular as "Cleanse Me."

Cleanse Me

Words: J. Edwin Orr
Music: Clement Scott, arr. R. J. Stevens

G - 2 - MI

The Guilty: A Worship Study

"You know," I said, "The last verse of 'Cleanse Me' originally said, 'O Holy Ghost, revival comes from Thee.' What do we think about that?" The murmurs of discontent I fully expected ensued.

"It's not so much the idea of the 'Holy Ghost' that bothers me," said Denise. "I'm not crazy about the term, and I'm glad most other versions call Him the Holy Spirit. Ghost, Spirit, whatever. But I'm put off a bit by the idea of the Holy Spirit, whatever you want to call Him, starting a revival. It sounds a bit too Charismatic for me—especially when you put it together with being filled with fire in verse 2. The Spirit's presence in us doesn't inform us today separate from the written word." Most everyone showed their agreement with Denise.

"But verse 4 goes on to emphasize the importance of the written word," I reply, feeling a bit contrarian. "Doesn't the Spirit inspire a revival in the people of God when they read the Bible?"

"Absolutely," said Denise, not backing down. "But notice, the word isn't given credit for the revival, per se—just the supplying of our need. And then it sounds like the "Lord" in the last line is referring to the Holy Spirit. Is that Scriptural? Is the Spirit ever called Lord?"

"I don't think so. But the Godhead stands as one. Maybe calling one Lord is the same as calling the rest Lord as well."

"Maybe. Nevertheless, I like it much better the way I learned it, with 'O Lord above' used instead. The whole thing ties together better when we don't bounce around from subject to subject. God saves us from sins, searches our hearts through the word to find impurities, encourages us to do better, and uses us to accomplish great things as individuals and as members of the church."

"Is it a depressing thing to sing about our sins and our need for cleansing?" I asked.

"I don't think so," Denise offered. "Not as long as we are getting the cleansing. If we aren't getting the cleansing, if we have to stay in our sins because of our refusal to repent, now that's something to be depressed about."

"Amen to that," I said.

What does "Cleanse Me" mean to you?
_____
_____
_____

The Bible Study Song List

If you were putting a list together for a study about guilt, what songs would you include and why? _____
_____
_____

What songs might you exclude and why? _____
_____
_____

Psalm 52
A Song for the Enemy

It is fascinating how frequently the Bible addresses itself to people who have little or no interest in reading it. Obadiah chastens the Edomites. Jesus pronounced "woes" against the Scribes and Pharisees and directly followed them by His lament that they refused to accept the shelter of His wings (Matthew 23). Ezekiel is told directly how stubborn and rebellious his audience will be before he even begins to prophesy (Ezekiel 2:1-5).

Such is also the case with many of the imprecatory psalms. The "hero" of Psalm 52 (likely a title given by the "hero" himself or by the psalmist in an attitude of sarcasm) is too busy basking in the joys of his evil lifestyle to worry about God's impression of him. And yet God not only condemns him, but He also does so in written form for all the world to see and then preserves it providentially for succeeding generations to see as well. Why go to so much trouble to condemn an absent audience?

One answer is that the assurance of evil's downfall encourages the faithful. The victims of his treachery need to remember that God sees all and that He will recompense in due course of time. As verses 6-7 remind us, we will be privileged to see victory over evil even within our lifetimes. Perhaps not in the case of every single blasphemer and heretic, but it will happen enough times to remind us not to envy the one who "trusted in the abundance of his riches, taking refuge in his destructive behavior."

¹ Why brag about evil, you hero!
God's faithful love is constant.
² Like a sharpened razor,
your tongue devised destruction,
working treachery.
³ You love evil instead of good,
lying instead of speaking truthfully.
Selah.
⁴ You love any words that destroy,
you treacherous tongue!
⁵ This is why God will bring you down forever.
He will take you, ripping you out of your tent;
He will uproot you from the land of the living. *Selah.*
⁶ The righteous will look on with awe and will ridicule him:
⁷ "Here is the man
who would not make God his refuge
but trusted in the abundance of his riches,
taking refuge in his destructive behavior."
⁸ I will praise You forever for what You have done.
In the presence of Your faithful people,
I will put my hope in Your name, for it is good.

A second answer is a bit more optimistic. Despite all appearances to the contrary, evil people do occasionally turn away from their evil even when they expressly refuse to do so time after time. Nineveh repented at the preaching of Jonah (Jonah 3:6-9). In doing so, they provided a warning to those who would repeat its oppressive and blasphemous ways (Matthew 12:41). Acts 2 records how 3,000 such souls, who had rejected "something greater than Jonah," were moved to repent at the preaching of Peter and the apostles at Pentecost.

A third answer is found in the aftermath of the promised downfall of the wicked. Perhaps the evil ones will persist in their wickedness and ultimately be brought down. Their downfall is not always fatal; sometimes evil ones are blessed to find themselves in possession of a second chance that they did not know they needed but which they suddenly appreciate more than life itself.

In any event, the ultimate conquest of evil is a recurring theme in the Bible. By faith, we accept the inequities of life, including the short-term victories of our enemies, will in the end be countered by an all-seeing and all-powerful God. Defeat is inevitable for the rebel, despite his bombast. In time, he will realize he never had reason to brag about anything. The faithful will in victory remember Jeremiah 9:24—"But the one who boasts should boast in this, that he understands and knows Me—that I am the LORD, showing faithful love, justice, and righteousness on the earth, for I delight in these things. This is the LORD's declaration."

1. Why might we be moved to doubt God's "faithful love" in times of oppression? _____
_____
_____

2. Give some examples from today's culture how wicked people boast about doing evil. _____
_____
_____

3. Verse 9 reads, "I will praise You forever for what You have done." For what specifically should we be praising God in the context of Psalm 52? _____
_____
_____

> **Figure of Speech**
>
> **A Sharpened Razor**
>
> A razor is not a large tool. Its steel is not generally any stronger than the steel you find elsewhere. But when sharpened to a fine edge, minimal effort applied in optimal fashion can produce maximum results.
>
> Such is the case with the tongue. A bold charge, or even a subtle word well placed, can devastate one's reputation. Using a different metaphor, "Consider how large a forest a small fire ignites" (James 3:5).
>
> A man puts his life in the hands of his barber when he asks him for a shave. He puts himself in similar straits when he confesses sins to him (James 5:16). Gossip is such a hurtful thing because it is a betrayal of the deepest trust. Such an injury may wind up doing irreparable damage. We should not be discouraged from believing all things, per 1 Corinthians 13:7; it should, though, remind us how precious and fragile our reputations are and how fiercely we should protect them.

4. What is your favorite line in the psalm and why? _____
_____
_____

The Enemy: A Bible Study

From Ahab's perspective, Elijah was the enemy. After all, Ahab had successfully negotiated a treaty with the Sidonians, sealing the deal by marrying Ethbaal's daughter, Jezebel, and institutionalizing the worship of Baal, the god from whom the names of both king and princess were derived. Elijah had not only protested this treaty but had brought down the wrath of God upon the entire nation. By the time Elijah finally presented himself to Ahab, the land had gone three years without rain (1 Kings 17:1). It is no wonder Ahab considered Elijah the "destroyer of Israel" (1 Kings 18:17).

Elijah responded in the next verse, "I have not destroyed Israel, but you and your father's house have, because you have abandoned the LORD's commandments and followed the Baals." The problem was not with the messenger or his message; it was with the sin that had prompted the message in the first place.

Doing the right thing often brings negative consequences—especially to the wrongdoer, but not exclusively so. Paul asks his brethren in Galatians 4:16,

"Have I now become your enemy by telling you the truth?" The "truth," as it happened, condemned many of the Galatians for accepting the false doctrine of the Judaizers. Despite Paul's warnings, some had accepted the teaching of those who said one could only receive salvation by adding their faith in Jesus to a strict adherence to the Law of Moses. These were the true enemies, and Paul condemned them in the harshest of tones—"I wish those who are disturbing you might also get themselves castrated!" (Galatians 5:12). Rejecting the false teacher may bring upon the church intense trouble and sorrow, making life harrowing for the faithful and the rebellious alike. Such factions are a necessary part of standing for the truth (1 Corinthians 11:18); one cannot sit idly by in the name of peace and allow false doctrine to carry the day.

It requires faith to stand up against the enemy in the face of public opposition and even personal suffering. God's partnership with Elijah is testimony that God is always with us and attentive to our needs even when it seems it is not the case. By praying for drought and rain, respectively, within the will of God, Elijah showed himself to be a faithful servant and trustworthy witness. Additionally, both his contemporaries and we as readers are reminded of the importance of prayer (James 5:17-18)—not as a vehicle for personal prominence or gain, but rather as a means of participating in the administration of God's will in this life.

Read Psalm 52 again—this time with Ahab in mind.

1. How relevant are "good intentions" when rebelling against God's will? _____
   _____
   _____
   _____

2. How should we respond when the evil tactics of the enemy achieve the exact good he had intended? What if most of our neighbors join in his celebration?
   _____
   _____
   _____
   _____

Psalm 94—A Parallel Study

Are the "stupid people" in Psalm 94:8 those who gloat over their evil deeds, or those who lose their faith when they do not see God's vengeance shown in what they would consider a timely and appropriate way? One can make a good argument for either. As the psalmist explains, the literal Inventor of hearing and seeing is more than aware of the events happening on the earth. Nothing escapes His notice. The ally of God can take great comfort in knowing this; the enemy of God should take great pause.

American Christians have been taught to trust the government and the Constitution to preserve our rights, particularly the rights of speech, assembly, and the practice of religion. Verse 20 warns us about trusting too much in "a corrupt throne"—and the "throne" in the immediate context seems to refer to the king of Israel, who surely could have been reasonably expected to treat God's people well. The bottom line is, humans are fallible, as are human governments. We certainly hope that our government sides with God and His people in opposition to the evils of this world, but we should not count on it or panic if we do not get it.

1. How important is vengeance? Should we pray for it—and if so, how? _____
_____
_____
_____

2. In what form does opposition from our enemies come today? What forms do you see on the horizon? How should we respond? _____
_____
_____
_____

3. Does the psalmist have specific "thoughts" in mind in verse 11? Why are they "meaningless?" _____
_____
_____
_____

4. What is your favorite line in the psalm and why? _____
_____
_____
_____

The Enemy: A Case Study

Avery had faithfully served as an overseer for almost ten years without any semblance of impropriety. He regularly golfed and lunched with the other elders and Eric, their local preacher. Religious discussions were more the rule than the exception. So it was a considerable surprise to them all, and to the rest of the congregation, when he asked for pulpit time one Sunday morning and preached what he claimed to have "always" believed about marriage, divorce and remarriage. The timing was not lost on Eric,

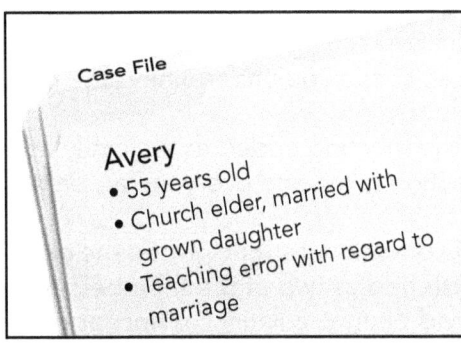

Case File

Avery
- 55 years old
- Church elder, married with grown daughter
- Teaching error with regard to marriage

who two weeks earlier had addressed the topic (and taught something quite different).

Avery took the position the definition of "divorced for the cause of fornication" was somewhat open to debate concerning those whose spouse had left the marriage for reasons other than an affair and then later remarried. "I am not suggesting that Brother Eric's position was wrong, mind you," he said. "I'm just saying the law is unclear, and we should take care not to bind where the Lord has not bound."

For the benefit of those who had not heard both lessons, Eric felt compelled to follow Avery into the pulpit. He reiterated in brief his position—a legally divorced person after several years could not reasonably "put away" a spouse (former spouse, more accurately) under any circumstances. He also brought up a subject he had intentionally avoided in his previous sermon—Avery's divorced daughter in another state was planning to marry again, and her first husband had divorced her for reasons other than fornication.

"Frankly, Avery, I have as much of a problem with the way this issue has been handled as I do with the doctrine itself," said one of the other elders that afternoon in a meeting with Avery and the other elders. "This is not an issue of immediate concern to the church here. You didn't talk to Eric or us about it beforehand. Personally, I'm stunned that you hold this position, and I have trouble avoiding the notion that this is a reality you have come up with purely to rationalize your daughter's marriage." The others agreed, and no effort on Avery's part seemed to change their minds.

"I won't argue with you," said Avery, stating the obvious, "this subject hits close to home. And yes, I have trouble with the preacher taking pot shots at my family. I am not going to try to split the church over this, naturally. But as an elder of this church, I am not going to sit idly by and listen to personal opinions preached as though they are grounded in Scripture."

"Then, as much as it pains me to say," said the elder, "perhaps you shouldn't be overseeing the church. The rest of us agree with Eric on this topic, and we can't have you undermining the credibility of the eldership."

The meeting ended as amicably as could have been expected, with no formal action taken and everyone agreeing to study and pray further.

Two weeks later, Eric invited the elders (Avery excepted) to his house. There they listened as two of the members repeated what they had told Eric—that Avery had been circulating rumors about Eric and, at least, one of the other elders, with the clear intention of getting Eric fired and the eldership either dissolved or rendered silent on the subject of divorce.

Read Psalm 52 again — this time with Avery in mind.

What would you say to Avery based on Psalm 52? _____
_____
_____
_____

New Testament Insight

> LORD, happy is the man You discipline
> and teach from Your law
> to give him relief from troubled times
> until a pit is dug for the wicked. — *Psalm 94:13-14*

The idea of discipline may seem out of place in a psalm written to chasten the enemies of God and assure His people of His vengeance against them. Primarily written for the faithful, Psalm 94 assures us our confidence in Him is well placed.

Discipline is thought of in a negative context, as with the discipline exercised by a parent toward an unruly child. However, "discipline" is from the same root as "disciple," and is simply a form of teaching. So we should not think of it necessarily as a bad thing. In fact, we read in Hebrews 12:3-12 (and in Proverbs 3:11-12, which is quoted by the Hebrews writer) that it is an expression of God's love for us and His desire that we grow and develop in the way He desires.

The hard times that come to us in life, often through the agency of evildoers, can be used to our advantage. Instead of whining about how unfairly treated we are in this life (as though we ever expected fairness from the world), we should allow the testing of our faith to work endurance in us (James 1:2-4).

Discipline can hurt, just like efforts to strengthen tired hands and weakened knees can. As the saying goes, "No pain, no gain." Trying to avoid pain in life may cost us a learning experience God wanted us to have.

The Enemy: A Hymn Study

First, there was a tune circulating in the revival meeting circuit in the early 1800s. One line in the verse would be repeated three times, followed by the second. *Oh! Brothers, will you meet me/Oh! Brothers, will you meet me/Oh! Brothers, will you meet me/On Canaan's happy shore?* Then the chorus: *There we'll shout and give Him glory,/There we'll shout and give Him glory,/There we'll shout and give Him glory/For glory is His own.* The well-known tune was co-opted by Northern troops in the War Between the States as a tribute to dead abolitionist John Brown and an anthem to the anti-slavery cause: *John Brown's body lies a-mouldering in the grave/His soul is marching on.*

The Battle Hymn of the Republic

Words: Julia Ward Howe
Music: American Folk Melody

B♭ - 4 - SOL

Julia Ward Howe was a staunch abolitionist whose husband, Samuel, was a member of the Secret Six, an organization that funded John Brown's work. When she heard the song at a public review of the troops in Washington, she thought the new lyrics too undignified for the noble purpose of the song and its Bible-based origins. She awoke early in the morning of November 18, 1861, with the song virtually completed in her head. Later she wrote, "I scrawled the verses almost without looking at the paper."

Her lyrics effectively used the imagery of the battlefield to depict not just the fight against rebellion and slavery but also the greater fight of the people of God against the devil and his agents. Her original line in the fifth stanza—"As He died to make men holy, let us die to make men free"—is often rewritten to have us "live to make men free" instead, an equally noble sentiment.

It is impossible to catalog the impact entirely "The Battle Hymn of the Republic" has had on American culture. As a theme for American pride and freedom, it has been used at numerous political conventions and inaugurations. It was played at the funerals of Richard Nixon, Ronald Reagan, and Winston Churchill, as well as the memorial for the fallen on September 14, 2001. The Mormon Tabernacle Choir's recording hit #13 on the Billboard Hot 100 and won the Grammy Award for Best Performance by a Vocal Group or Chorus in 1960. Andy Williams' performance at Robert Kennedy's funeral reached #33, #11 on the adult contemporary chart. Its lyrics provided the titles to John Steinbeck's *The Grapes of Wrath*, John Updike's *In the Beauty of the Lilies*, and Bruce Catton's *Never Sound Retreat* and *Terrible Swift Sword*. Dr. Martin Luther King's final public speech ended with the words, "Mine eyes have seen the glory of the coming of the Lord."

The Enemy: A Worship Study

"Is it safe to sing this hymn?" I asked the group, which skewed decidedly Southern. "After all, it's only been a century and a half since the war."

"I think so," said Enid with a relatively high degree of confidence. "Slavery was wrong. We all realize that now. We may not all agree with the war or some of the tactics taken in it, but I can't see how anyone would have an issue with us asking God to help our fellow humans be treated as souls made in the image of God."

"And 'The Battle Hymn of the Republic' is not really about the war at all for most people who sing it today," Emory suggested. "It's another warfare hymn, like 'Faith is the Victory' or 'The Battle Belongs to the Lord.' God is fighting against sin, and He is asking us to join with Him."

"And I think that's the main point of this hymn," I said. "It's 'the glory of the coming of the Lord' that we have seen. This is God's fight, not ours."

"I have to say," Elijah interjected, "I'm not totally persuaded about the spiritual nature of this so-called hymn. We are authorized to sing 'psalms, hymns, and spiritual songs' in worship, according to Colossians 3:16. But isn't this one more about politics than the cause of Christ?"

"Well, the people of that day certainly would not have thought so," I responded. "Rightly or wrongly, they saw themselves as God's warriors doing God's bidding."

"But that doesn't mean they were right in so doing," Elijah persisted.

"No, it doesn't. And I understand your point; the song is certainly political. But military imagery is often used to describe a spiritual conflict; the book of Revelation is full of it. Just because Julia Ward Howe pictured Jesus as going to war against the South when she wrote about "burnished rows of steel' doing His bidding, how He would 'crush the serpent (meaning the South) with His heel' — that doesn't mean I have to mean that when I sing her song."

Elijah shrugged. "I don't know. Maybe there's just too much Southern boy in me to see that song as anything but insulting."

"Well, as a fellow Southern boy, I don't entirely disagree with you. But I think we can all agree that Jesus is at war with the sinful aspects of our culture and we fight with Him when we oppose them. We can argue all day about whether slavery is or was inherently sinful; back in the day, they had week-long debates on the subject and never resolved anything as far as I can tell. But there's no doubt that humans perpetrated awful, unrighteousness against other humans simply because of the color of their skin. Even today, at least to some extent, we are still battling to make sure basic human dignity is extended to everyone. And that's absolutely God's fight."

"I couldn't agree more," said Ethan.

What does "The Battle Hymn of the Republic" mean to you? _____
_____
_____

The Bible Study Song List

If you were putting a list together for a study about the enemy, what songs would you include and why? _____
_____

What songs might you exclude and why? _____
_____

Psalm 59
A Song for the Persecuted

Somehow, some way, we picked up the notion that life was supposed to be fair—that mean people were mean because they didn't understand us correctly, or because someone treated them poorly. Surely if we abide by the Golden Rule, others will do the same, right?

Unfortunately, we learn before too long in this world that there are ugly, hateful, despicable people out there. It has nothing to do with our behavior and values; if anything, they are even more ugly toward us when they realize what we believe.

We set ourselves up for failure, though, when we assume God's job is to remove our persecutors from our lives. Although He often does providentially clear the path for us temporarily, persecution is a part of our lives as Christians (2 Timothy 3:12). In fact, Jesus says in Matthew 5:11-12 that persecution can be a blessing; surely He would not want to rob us of a blessing, nor should we wish Him to do so.

The deliverance God offers is not the immediate, complete and permanent removal of all problems or any particular problem. The deliverance God offers is found in faith. When we lean on the Lord more when we need Him more, we are reminded of His presence in our lives at all times. He provides a shield (v.11) to ward off the attacks that will continue to come our way.

¹ Deliver me from my enemies, my God;
protect me from those who rise up against me.
² Deliver me from those who practice sin,
and save me from men of bloodshed.
³ LORD, look! They set an ambush for me.
Powerful men attack me,
but not because of any sin or rebellion of mine.
⁴ For no fault of mine,
they run and take up a position.
Awake to help me, and take notice.
⁵ LORD God of Hosts, You are the God of Israel,
rise up to punish all the nations;
do not show grace to any wicked traitors. *Selah*
⁶ They return at evening, snarling like dogs
and prowling around the city.
⁷ Look, they spew from their mouths—
sharp words from their lips.
"For who," they say, "will hear?"
⁸ But You laugh at them, LORD;
You ridicule all the nations.
⁹ I will keep watch for You, my strength,
because God is my stronghold.

¹⁰ My faithful God will come to
    meet me;
  God will let me look down on
    my adversaries.
¹¹ Do not kill them; otherwise, my
    people will forget.
  By Your power, make them
    homeless wanderers
  and bring them down,
    Lord, our shield.
¹² For the sin of their mouths and
    the words of their lips,
  let them be caught in their pride.
  They utter curses and lies.
¹³ Consume them in rage;
  consume them until they are
    gone.
  Then people will know through-
    out the earth
  that God rules over Jacob. *Selah*
¹⁴ And they return at evening,
    snarling like dogs
  and prowling around the city.
¹⁵ They scavenge for food;
  they growl if they are not
    satisfied.
¹⁶ But I will sing of Your strength
  and will joyfully proclaim
  Your faithful love in the morning.
  For You have been a stronghold
    for me,
  a refuge in my day of trouble.
¹⁷ To You, my strength, I sing
    praises,
  because God is my stronghold—
  my faithful God.

Our strength will not win the day; it is His (v.16). Remember 1 John 4:4—"You are from God, little children, and you have conquered them, because the One who is in you is greater than the one who is in the world." As long as we maintain our faith, the battle has already been won. That knowledge will see us through the hours when we have trouble seeing His hand.

1. Name one or two specific categories of enemies we face in life. Does God grant us deliverance from them in this life? And if so, how? _____
_____
_____
_____
_____

2. Find a New Testament passage distinguishing between suffering for sin and suffering for righteousness. Is suffering noble in and of itself? Explain. _____
_____
_____
_____
_____
_____

3. Why does the psalmist not want God to kill his enemies? Explain why leaving them alive can be a greater blessing than removing them permanently. ___
_____
_____
_____
_____
_____

4. What is your favorite line in the psalm and why? _____
_____
_____
_____
_____
_____

> ## Figure of Speech
> ### Dogs
>
> We are used to thinking of dogs as pets, given to showing love and support, perhaps even trained to accomplish a task for the family. However, the Bible depicts dogs as wild beasts, given to scavenging and to attacking the weak and defenseless. Dogs were to be avoided because of the threats they posed to the health and safety of humans. The scavenging habit of "four-footed animals that walk on their paws" (Leviticus 11:27) were no doubt part of the rationale for tagging them as unclean under the Law of Moses.
>
> Dogs' inherently unclean lifestyle is depicted in their tendency to eat their own vomit (Proverbs 26:11, 2 Peter 2:22). Even house dogs were kept "under the table" (Mark 7:27-28) where they would get only what humans did not want.
>
> Because of the vicious nature of dogs, as well as their tendency to travel in packs, human detractors are often compared to dogs (Psalm 22:16; Isaiah 56:10; Philippians 3:2). They are excluded from decent company, including the glory awaiting the people of God (Revelation 22:15).

The Persecuted: A Bible Study

Jeremiah had ample reason to feel persecuted. Firstly, and primarily, his nation was in ruins. He describes in the first chapter of Lamentations how the Babylonians had laid waste of Jerusalem. Two previous waves of conquest had been nothing in comparison; the downfall in 586 B.C. included the collapse of Jerusalem's wall, the destruction of Solomon's temple, and the wholesale carnage that swallowed up even King Zedekiah. Verses 10-11 read, "The adversary has seized all her precious belongings. She has even seen the nations enter her sanctuary—those You had forbidden to enter Your assembly. All her people groan while they search for bread. They have traded their precious belongings for food in order to stay alive." But then, to make matters even worse for Jeremiah, he continues: "LORD, look and see how I have become despised." Somehow Jeremiah had come to be seen as part of the problem.

In fact, Jeremiah had tried desperately to be part of the solution. In Jeremiah 36, we read how Jeremiah dictated a scroll to his scribe, Baruch, and had it delivered to King Jehoiakim—only to have it shredded and burned. In Jeremiah 37, then-King Zedekiah vacillates wildly between asking Jeremiah for the word of God and throwing him in prison for giving it. In Jeremiah 38, Zedekiah's officials insist on throwing Jeremiah into a muddy cistern, while Zedekiah claims to be unable to stop them.

Finally, in Lamentations, Jeremiah is looking out at the destruction of which he prophesied—if only they had listened to God, He could have lessened the squalor and suffering. How fitting he should say in Lamentations 1:12, "Is this nothing to you, all you who pass by? Look and see! Is there any pain like mine, which was dealt out to me, which the LORD made me suffer on the day of His burning anger?" And again in verse 16, "I weep because of these things; my eyes flow with tears. For there is no one nearby to comfort me, no one to keep me alive. My children are desolate because the enemy has prevailed."

On and on his laments continue. But a strange thing happens as he reaches a climax in the middle of chapter 3. After emphasizing again in verses 19-20 the depth of his despair and how depressed he has become, he writes in verse 21, "Yet I call this to mind, and therefore I have hope." What could bring hope to a heart so broken?

Verses 22-25 give the answer. God's faithful love. His endless mercies. His unchanging faithfulness. Surely He is worthy of our hope, no matter what the circumstances may be.

The lesson for us is in verses 26-27—"The LORD is good to those who wait for Him, to the person who seeks Him. It is good to wait quietly for deliverance from the LORD." Being in the midst of hardships may blind us to God's love for us—and if we are honest, there may be a bit of self-pity in there as well. But by learning patience, by persisting in faith, by complaining less and praying more, we can find peace in the most adverse of circumstances.

Read Psalm 59 again—this time with Jeremiah in mind.

1. What does Jeremiah mean in Lamentations 3:27 by, "It is good for a man to bear the yoke while he is still young"? _____
_____
_____
_____

2. Why are we persecuted? Why do our enemies do it, and why does God allow it? _____
_____
_____
_____

Psalm 69— A Parallel Study

Thanks to the inspired books of the New Testament, we can see snippets of the life of Jesus scattered throughout the Old Testament—many of which we would never have seen without aid. Such is the case concerning the sufferings of Christ on the cross as portended in Psalm 69.

Aside from generalities about opposition to Himself and His righteous cause, we are given specifics about His treatment on the cross. Verse 21 reads, "…they gave me gall for my food, and for my thirst they gave me vinegar to drink." Although the text does not cite the passage as having been fulfilled, as is the case with many prophecies, Matthew 27:34 specifically mentions gall as having been given to Jesus, perhaps as a soporific to dull His pain (which would explain why He did not accept it). Also, vinegar, or "sour wine" (Matthew 27:48; John 19:19:29) was given to Him in a sponge in response to His cry "I'm thirsty!"—itself apparently a reference to a clearly Messianic text in Psalm 22:15.

1. How does Jesus' response to adversity help us in our hour of trial? _____
   _____
   _____

2. Find two instances in Jesus' life where He said, "A slave is not greater than His master." Explain the meaning of the saying and its relevance with regard to suffering. _____
   _____
   _____

3. Who are the ones who make up songs and stories about Jesus clearly intending to demean Him? Why do they do so and do people do the same today? ____
   _____
   _____

4. What is your favorite line in the psalm and why? _____
   _____
   _____

The Persecuted: A Case Study

"This is why I stopped making wedding cakes," Jill said, frustrated. "I saw all these cases in the news about homosexual couples pressuring bakeries with Christian values in to making cakes for their weddings, and I just didn't want to go down that road. I've turned away thousands of dollars in business over the last five years or so because I didn't want to have this conversation."

"And they know that," said Brenda, Jill's friend. Brenda, who worked the register at Jill's bakery, was the one who had the first conversation with the couple in question. After having ascertained that Jill did not make wedding cakes, they confirmed that she did do large batches of cookies for special events. Now it seemed they didn't want a "wedding cake" at all; they wanted large, individual cookies with their faces printed in icing on them, kissing, written below the picture the word "Forever."

"Of course, they know," Jill said. "They don't care about cookies. I suspect they don't even care about being married. This is just a naked attempt to drive me out of business. They saw my gospel meeting invitations on the counter, and they saw Scripture verses on my wall, and they decided I was a threat to them before they ever even met me."

"I've never seen someone bring a lawyer in to place an order before," Brenda said.

"That should tell you something right there."

"And I noticed they did not go to Mahmoud's, right across the street. He does wedding cakes and cookies. But nobody threatens his business by forcing him to renounce his values. And his cookies are just as good as yours. Well," she said upon receiving a withering glare, "almost as good."

"Kicking me when I'm down," Jill said, with wry humor. "Some friend you are."

Brenda walked over and hugged her friend. "We will get through this. I promise."

"Yes," Jill said, tearing up a bit, "but how?"

Read Psalm 59 again—this time with Jill in mind.

What would you say to Janet based on Psalm 59?

_____
_____
_____

New Testament Insight

I have become a stranger to my brothers
and a foreigner to my mother's sons,
because zeal for Your house has consumed me,
and the insults of those who insult You
have fallen on me.   — Psalm 69:8-9

Psalm 69 is a description of one who has given himself wholly to the pursuit of God's will in his life—a pursuit costing him dearly. Not only does he suffer because of public perception, but even his close family relationships have also suffered because he is so completely given over to the things of God.

Even if Psalm 69:9 were not quoted in the New Testament in the context of applying prophecy to Jesus, we would likely see the similarity. Jesus was estranged from His brothers (John 7:1-5), and His evident preference for His responsibilities to the gospel over family obligations (Matthew 12:46-50) very well may have been part of that. Rarely do we see any indication in the gospel record of Jesus occupying Himself with anything other than the task He assumed when He was just 12 years old—being "in My Father's house" (Luke 2:49).

As it happens, we are not left to speculate. His disciples were reminded of the passage when He drove the moneychangers out of the temple during His first visit during His ministry, saying, "Get these things out of here! Stop turning My Father's house into a marketplace!" (John 2:13-17). He made a similar display five days before His crucifixion, according to Matthew 21:12-13, Mark 11:5-18, and Luke 19:45-47.

The Persecuted: A Hymn Study

"We Gather Together" has come to be associated with Thanksgiving Day in America, with many churches singing it during services in the holiday season. In truth, though, other than the first line of the first stanza, the song has little to do with public gatherings or the giving of thanks—and certainly nothing to do with American history, the Pilgrims, or turkey dinners.

Dutch Protestants wrote the hymn while suffering at the hand of Spanish Catholics around the end of the 16th Century. King Philip II dominated much of Europe at the time. An uprising from the Dutch in 1566 brought swift reprisals from Philip; many Protestants, as well as Catholic sympathizers, were executed. But,

We Gather Together

1. We gath-er to-geth-er to ask the Lord's bless-ing;
He chas-tens and has-tens His will to make known;
The wick-ed op-press-ing now cease from dis-tress-ing.
Sing prais-es to his name; he fails not his own.

2. Be-side us to guide us, our God with us join-ing,
Or-dain-ing, main-tain-ing His king-dom di-vine;
So from the be-gin-ning the fight we were win-ning;
Thou, Lord, wast at our side— all glo-ry be Thine!

3. We all do ex-tol Thee, Thou King of the na-tions,
And pray that Thou still our De-fend-er wilt be.
Let Thy con-gre-ga-tion es-cape trib-u-la-tion;
Be Thou for-ev-er praised, Thou God of the free!

Words: Valerius' *Collection*, tr. Theodore Baker
Music: Valerius' *Collection*, arr. Edward Kremser, alt.

D - 3 - SOL

in what Protestants throughout Europe considered nothing less than an act of God, the Spanish Armada was destroyed by a series of remarkable events in 1588 while trying to invade England. Europe broke the stranglehold the Spanish had on them.

Around 1597, Dutch writer Adrianus Valerius penned the original words to "Wilt Heden Nu Treden" in anticipation of a new century that promised more freedom than they had ever known. It gave credit for earlier successes to God, thanking Him that "The wicked oppressing now cease from distressing," and asked Him for further help in the future.

Theodore Baker is credited with the English words to the hymn, which are not a literal translation from the Dutch. When the Dutch Reformed Church in America decided in 1937 to add modern hymns to their worship for the first time, "We Gather Together" was the first hymn chosen for its first hymnal.

The Persecuted: A Worship Study

"We sang 'We Gather Together' every Thanksgiving Day week when I was growing up," said Janis, a recent convert. "I never really took it seriously. In fact, my sisters and I made up lyrics that we thought were more appropriate." And she gave us a little concert to demonstrate:

> *We gather together for turkey and dressing,*
> *Cranberries and salad and Gran's pumpkin pie.*
> *Let cheering and clapping*
> *Not interrupt Dad's napping*
> *While Lions and Cowboys the day occupy.*

After the applause had died, I said, "You know, the Pilgrims' quest to escape persecution by coming to the New World is largely overblown. They had almost all the freedom they could ask for after relocating to the Netherlands."

"Then why did the Pilgrims sing the song, if they had already escaped tribulation?" Jamie wanted to know.

"The Pilgrims didn't write the song; Dutch Protestants a generation earlier did. And besides, I have never been able to confirm that the Pilgrims sang 'We Gather Together.' It's likely they did; I'm not saying they didn't. I'm just saying the idea that they sang this song hoping the New World would be easier on them than Mother England, that's largely a myth."

"Then why did they come here in the first place, if they had already found a comfortable home?"

"That's just it," I said. "For some, it was too comfortable. The Puritans of the early 17th Century didn't think it was right to live here in Satan's world without being persecuted. After all, 2 Timothy 3:12 states pretty clearly that godly people will suffer persecution. To entirely avoid the conflict that had characterized the previous generation in England was to diminish the commitment they were making to Christ."

"But the song says, 'Let Thy congregation escape tribulation,'" someone pointed out. "What about that?"

"Well, I don't speak Dutch, so I don't know how close to the original language the English version we know is. But I do know that escaping tribulation doesn't necessarily mean avoiding it. Sometimes what we need far more than relief from persecution is the strength to endure it. And sometimes, in God's wisdom, He decides to make us work for it."

What does "We Gather Together" mean to you? _____
_____
_____
_____

The Bible Study Song List

If you were putting a list together for a study about persecution, what songs would you include and why? _____
_____
_____
_____

What songs might you exclude and why? _____
_____
_____

Psalm 75
A Song for the Thankful

"For Your name is near" seems like an odd reason for giving thanks to God. Certainly there are hundreds of reasons to give Him the honor due Him. And yet this is the one the Holy Spirit chooses to give Asaph to begin Psalm 75.

The key to understanding the phrase is in knowing how the Bible uses the concept of names, and particularly the name of God. The name of God denotes His authority and power. We see this in expressions such as, "the place to have His name dwell" (Deuteronomy 12:11), "calling on His name" (Acts 22:16), "the name of the LORD is a strong tower" (Proverbs 18:11), etc. To honor His name is to honor Him; to trust in His name is to trust in Him.

His name is near to us in part because we make it so; we as His people seek out His presence and rejoice in it. But in the context of Psalm 78, His name, or demonstration of His presence, is near because He makes it so. He chooses the time (v.2). He establishes order (v.3). He humbles the prideful (v.4). And when we see Him in the world acting to exalt His name—whether simply by maintaining the marvelous creation He put in place initially, or by in some small way reminding us that He rules in the kingdoms of men — we are prompted again to give Him thanks.

1 We give thanks to You, God;
we give thanks to You, for Your name is near.
People tell about Your wonderful works.
2 "When I choose a time,
I will judge fairly.
3 When the earth and all its inhabitants shake,
I am the One who steadies its pillars.   *Selah.*
4 I say to the boastful, 'Do not boast,'
and to the wicked, 'Do not lift up your horn.
5 Do not lift up your horn against heaven
or speak arrogantly.'"
6 Exaltation does not come
from the east, the west, or the desert,
7 for God is the judge:
He brings down one and exalts another.
8 For there is a cup in the LORD's hand,
full of wine blended with spices,
and He pours from it,
all the wicked of the earth will drink,
draining it to the dregs.
9 As for me, I will tell about Him forever;
I will sing praise to the God of Jacob.
10 "I will cut off all the horns of the wicked,
but the horns of the righteous will be lifted up."

The strongest affirmations of God's sovereignty in the psalm are reserved for the aspects that we do not yet see. According to verses 6-8, He is the ultimate arbiter of justice and punishment in the world. Instead of looking to the horizon for a conquering hero to ride in and set things right, "God is the judge; He brings down one and exalts another." The Babylonians would arise to supplant the Assyrians, and the Persians to supplant the Babylonians, and on and on throughout history, but the sentence of death was passed down from a court far higher than any court of man.

The cup in God's hand is an image common to both Old and New Testament passages. Drinking the cup of His wrath induces more than a stupor passing with a night's rest; the one cursed to drink will do so to his destruction—generally permanent destruction.

Although the enemies of God come and go, His people remain. We use our time in His presence to sing His praises as the One, the only One, who deserves our ultimate trust and faithfulness. So then, "we give thanks to You, for Your name is near" means, basically, "Thank You for being God." And we do thank Him. Who else could do what He does? "Proclaim with me the LORD's greatness; let us exalt His name together" (Psalm 34:3).

1. What is implied in the statement in verse 2 that God chooses the time to act, not we ourselves? _____
   _____
   _____
   _____

2. What sort of boasting might the rebellious soul engage in, bringing on God's condemnation and wrath? _____
   _____
   _____
   _____

3. Find several other passages describing God's enemies drinking from His cup of wrath. What does the expression mean to you? _____
   _____
   _____
   _____

4. What is your favorite line in the psalm and why? _____
   _____
   _____
   _____

> **Figure of Speech**
>
> ### Lift Up Your Horn
>
> Animal horns, especially ram's horns, have been used for millennia as musical instruments. The word has adapted over the years in meaning to refer to the musical instrument itself; trumpets, trombones and other wind instruments are frequently called "horns" even when made of a material other than animal horns.
>
> The horn was blown to give a signal over a long distance, particularly in battle. The blowing of horns signified an attack, perhaps most notably in the stories of Gideon (Judges 7:22) and of Joshua's attack on Jericho (Joshua 6:20). So the lifting up of the horn came to represent the beginning of a battle.
>
> Horns also refer to powerful forces in prophetic texts (Daniel 7:7, Revelation 12:3). As a ram does battle by lifting up his horns to attack his opponent, so also a mighty king might be depicted either by a horn or an animal bearing horns. Such horns can be extremely dangerous in an attack—but not, of course, to God, who has power much mightier than anything any human or human kingdom may bring to bear.

The Thankful: A Bible Study

The conflict between Jews and Samaritans in the First Century was palpable. Very real animosity existed on both sides. The Jews resented the Samaritans' historically flighty (at best) connection to the God of heaven. The Samaritans resented the Jews constantly treating them as spiritual inferiors. Both would go to considerable measures to avoid contact with the other.

Of course, that goes out the window when they both have leprosy.

The ten lepers whom Jesus found in Luke 17:11-19 were social outcasts. Not only were they ceremonially unclean, and thus unfit on an official basis; they were unacceptable in virtually any social setting. Although the disease we know today as leprosy is only mildly contagious and spreads between humans with difficulty, it is widely thought that leprosy in the Bible refers to a full gamut of skin afflictions. Leviticus 13-14 goes into some detail explaining the differences between them, which ones were unclean and which ones were not, and the quarantine procedures appropriate in the case of serious afflictions. In extreme circumstances, which obviously was the case here, they were to be ostracized from society until a priest examined the disease and determined the leper to be safe.

The social constructs separating Jews and Samaritans in health did not seem to matter much to the ten lepers. On the surface, at least, it seemed they had far more points of commonality than points of difference. There is a fellowship in misery.

Sin, of course, is the affliction that should concern us the most—an affliction of the soul and not the flesh, an affliction shutting us away from anything of spiritual value, including and especially fellowship with God. Because Jesus has come into our lives and saved us by grace through faith (Ephesians 2:4-5), we can be pure and holy in His sight and enjoy the privileges that come with being a child of God.

Just because we are promised it, just because we expect it, doesn't mean we don't have to thank Him. We read in 1 Thessalonians 5:18, "Give thanks in everything, for this is God's will for you in Christ Jesus." Surely "everything" must include forgiveness of sins—the greatest gift of all.

If we are not careful, we as Christians can become so accustomed to the idea of forgiveness and fellowship that we think of it as our due. We forget that our sin is as great as anyone else's, including the sin we commit after finding and accepting Christ.

It very well might be that a foreigner to the faith, one who has never known true fellowship in Jesus, might be more genuine in his thanksgiving than an experienced Christian, who merely attaches "Forgive us of our sins" to the end of every prayer by rote and gives the matter no more thought.

It might be. But it shouldn't be.

Read Psalm 75 again—this time with the leper in mind.

1. Other than literally giving thanks in prayer, what can we do to show our gratitude to the Lord for what He has done for us? _____
   _____
   _____
   _____

2. Explain what Jesus meant when He said, "Your faith has made you well." ___
   _____
   _____
   _____

Psalm 136—A Parallel Study

Even devoted Bible students will unlikely identify Psalm 136 without turning pages. When they do turn pages and find it, they are likely to say something akin to, "Oh, I remember—the repetitive one." Perhaps we would prefer a bit less repetition. Given our own culture's fondness for music lyrics that are not much less repetitive than this, perhaps we should be surprised we don't have more psalms written this way—and certainly we should be tolerant of this one and its eccentricity.

Surely God had a reason for giving us the psalm in the form He chose. The most obvious answer is in every chapter of their history God demonstrated His love for His people. From the dawn of creation to the Exodus to the conquest of Canaan, God proved Himself over and over to be not only the great and mighty One but also the compassionate, supportive and rewarding One. Perhaps that is a song that bears repeating.

His love is eternal. His love is eternal. His love is eternal. His love is eternal.

1. How has God shown His love for you throughout your life? _____
_____
_____
_____

2. What does it mean to be "God of gods" and "Lord of lords" (v.2-3)? _____
_____
_____
_____

3. What does it mean to you to have the "eternal" love of God? _____
_____
_____
_____

4. What is your favorite line in the psalm and why? _____
_____
_____
_____

The Thankful: A Case Study

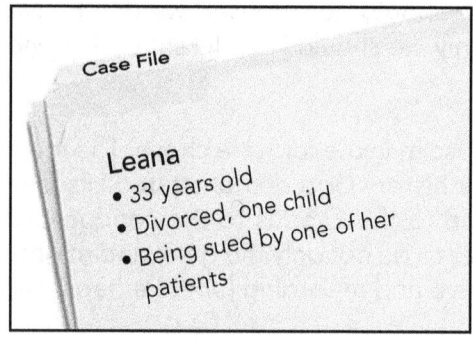

Case File

Leana
- 33 years old
- Divorced, one child
- Being sued by one of her patients

Leana was a constant source of encouragement to everyone in the congregation. Abandoned by an unfaithful husband as soon as his law school was paid for, she was left to put herself through her schooling to become a nurse practitioner with full-time custody of Leo, who was two at the time. She never complained, never seemed to harbor resentment. Thanks to a lot of long hours, a lot of prayers, and a lot of free child care from the members, she was able to graduate with honors and was quickly snatched up by a local medical group.

Now, after five years of hard work and building relationships, she was being sued by one of her patients. Her colleagues had been supportive at first; now it was beginning to appear that the partners' best chance at keeping the doors open was to cut Leana loose.

"It's not fair," Leana said, stating the obvious in an uncharacteristic display of temper. "I've given five years to that company. Where's the gratitude? Where's the appreciation?"

"So the lawsuit is just harassment?" a friend asked.

"That's it. And I'm sure it will go away in time. But for now, I have to pay legal bills. And I'm not likely to find any income with this hanging over my head."

"Is there anything at all we can do?"

Leana smiled weakly. "Do you have a spare $100,000?"

"No, really," she quickly added as her friend was obviously uncomfortable. "Keep praying for us, certainly. The brethren have been so encouraging to me and Leo over the years, and I am so grateful. I hope I don't sound otherwise right now. But in all honesty, it's a bit difficult to see the positive in things these days.

Read Psalm 75 again—this time with Leana in mind.

What would you say to Leana based on Psalm 75? _____
_____
_____
_____

New Testament Insight

And gave their land as an inheritance,
   His love is eternal,
an inheritance to Israel His servant.
   His love is eternal.   — *Psalm 136:21-22*

When God spoke to Abraham in Haran (Genesis 12:1) and even before that in Mesopotamia (Acts 7:2-3), He promised to show him a land. If He had not made it evident this land was for Abraham and his family, He did so in Genesis 13:15. The promise of a land to call his own was an assurance God gave to Abraham (and, in turn, to Isaac and Jacob) that his future was secure.

The inheritance Israel received in Canaan realized in the days of Joshua (Joshua 11:23) was only a foretaste of the true blessing to come—a place the people of God would call their own not only for a lifetime or the lifetime of their descendants but all of eternity. That assurance kept the patriarchs confident in their day (Hebrews 11:13-16), and it will keep us confident as well while we wait for the heavenly city God has prepared for us.

When Jesus made reference to our inheritance in Matthew 5:5—"Blessed are the gentle, because they will inherit the earth"—He was not speaking of a literal, physical inheritance. He meant His followers, by meekly accepting God at His word and waiting for Him to deliver, would inherit not only a parcel of land but rather absolutely everything there could ever be to receive.

The Patient: A Hymn Study

Johnson Oatman Jr., the writer of "Count Your Blessings," did not begin writing hymns until he was 36, although he was active in various churches all his life. He was ordained a Methodist minister but felt the call to expand his efforts beyond a single congregation. Eventually, his quest for the right way to use his talents led him to hymn writing. Within three years, hundreds of his hymns had already acquired widespread usage. He went on to write more than 5,000 hymns over the next 25 years, including "Higher Ground," "Hand in Hand with Jesus," "I'll Be a Friend to Jesus," and his personal favorite, "No, Not One."

Despite his popularity, he refused to use hymn writing as a way to earn money, choosing instead to earn money through secular work. When publishers insisted on paying him for his work, he would accept no more than $1 per hymn.

The idea of counting blessings appears to have resonated in American musical culture in the early part of the 20th Century. Reginald Morgan and Edith Temple released a song by that title in 1946 which has been re-recorded several times. Irving Berlin's "Count Your Blessings (Instead of Sheep)" was sung by Bing Crosby and Rosemary Clooney in the film classic *White Christmas.* Metro-Goldwyn-

Count Your Blessings

Psalm 75—A Song for the Thankful | 123

Words: Johnson Oatman, Jr.
Music: Edwin O. Excell

E♭ - 2 - MI

Mayer released *Count Your Blessings*, starring Deborah Kerr and Maurice Chevalier, in 1959. But Oatman's classic hymn predated them all, perhaps informed them all, and certainly has endured better and touched more lives than them all.

The Thankful: A Worship Study

"I would be interested to hear if anyone has ever, literally, tried to count their blessings," I asked after singing the old standard exhorting us to do just that. Several hands went up.

"I don't know if I ever put a number on it," Lincoln said, "but one day when I was about 12, and I had been acting up, my dad told me to go in my room and count my blessings. And when I took the assignment seriously and started thinking about all the things God does for me every day, it hit home." Several others in the group nodded their heads, evidently having experienced the same thing.

"I counted them one time," Lara said. "I stopped at 321. And that was just because I fell asleep."

"How did that happen?" everyone wanted to know.

"I was being a brat," Lara said. "I was 16, and Mom had grounded me from the car. I put on my best pouty face and started complaining about how nothing ever worked out for me. And Mom made me go to my room and write down 50 things I had to be thankful for, and why. It was tough. It took me about two hours. I put down the usual generalities—the Bible, the church, my family, that sort of thing.

"Then, when I gave the list to Mom, she said, 'Now do 50 more.' That made me mad. I said I would never think of 50 more. She promised me that I would, and said I could be more specific with the ones I had already chosen. I just had to explain how each item got on the list. So I mentioned every book of the Bible I could get specific about, every friend, and so on. It only took me half an hour. And it was weird; I felt less frustrated than after I finished the first 50.

"Then she challenged me to do 100 more. I started getting specific about the things my friends do for me, specific flowers and trees, even the 'tough love' Mom and Dad gave me. I kept going all evening. I finally fell asleep with 321 things listed.

"When I woke up in the morning, I took my list to Mom and showed her, and I apologized for being so horrible."

"Did you get ungrounded?" I asked.

"Nope," she said. We all laughed.

What does "Count Your Blessings" mean to you? _____
_____
_____
_____

The Bible Study Song List

If you were putting a list together for a study about thankfulness, what songs would you include and why? _____
_____
_____
_____

What songs might you exclude and why? _____
_____
_____

Psalm 91
A Song for Life

Throughout the history of Israel, circumstances persuaded the king to put his reliance on another, stronger king. He would make an alliance with, say, the Assyrians, thinking the power wielded by the king would be sufficient to secure the nation (and the king) in the coming days. Such protection was not sought from a lesser king, naturally; what purpose would that serve? It wasn't just a matter of being a few fighters short; the king needed support from a source significantly stronger than himself, and he typically was willing to pay dearly to get it.

Tragically, such kings failed to realize the access they already had to such a King—a King far stronger than all of his enemies put together. The shield He was able to provide was more than a military advantage; He promised to protect from the ravage of enemies, physical afflictions, poor fortune, wild animals, and perhaps even his own hubris. To turn away from such a help in favor of an earthly leader—and likely even incur the wrath of the truly powerful One—would seem completely unthinkable.

The absence of faith does that. Moments of weakness make us focus on immediate problems and search for immediate solutions. God does not always give the appearance of offering that. So we in our impatience work out a different plan, and in so doing assure our destruction instead of forestalling it.

¹ The one who lives under the protection of the Most High
dwells in the shadow of the Almighty.
² I will say to the LORD, "My refuge and my fortress,
my God, in whom I trust."
³ He Himself will deliver you from the hunter's net,
from the destructive plague.
⁴ He will cover you with His feathers:
you will take refuge under His wings.
His faithfulness will be a protective shield.
⁵ You will not fear the terror of the night,
the arrow that flies by day,
⁶ the plague that stalks in darkness,
or the pestilence that ravages at noon.
⁷ Though a thousand fall at your side
and ten thousand at your right hand
the pestilence will not reach you.
⁸ You will only see it with your eyes
and witness the punishment of the wicked.

⁹ Because you have made the LORD—
   my refuge,
   the Most High—your dwelling place,
¹⁰ no harm will come to you;
   no plague will come near your tent;
¹¹ For He will give His angels orders
      concerning you, to protect you
      in all your ways.
¹² They will support you with their hands
   so that you will not strike your foot
      against a stone.
¹³ You will tread on the lion and the
      cobra;
   you will trample the young lion and
      the serpent.
¹⁴ Because he is lovingly devoted to Me,
   I will deliver him;
   I will exalt him because he knows My
      name.
¹⁵ When he calls out to Me, I will answer
      him;
   I will be with him in trouble.
   I will rescue him and give him honor.
¹⁶ I will satisfy him with a long life
   and show him My salvation.

"The meaning of life" is not as complicated as it is made out to be, and comes into clear relief when we realize who we are, how we came to be thus, and why the world itself even exists. God made us in His image (Genesis 1:27). We are made to honor and serve Him (Ecclesiastes 12:13). A life spent avoiding such considerations, and their implications will inevitably seem empty and vain; Solomon eventually came to that conclusion after a lifetime of searching for other, different answers.

On the other hand, embracing the true nature of life under God's sun makes us all the more aware not only of our origin but also of our ongoing and multifaceted need for Him. We are glad, then, to put all of our eggs in His basket. "For you have died, and your life is hidden with the Messiah in God" (Colossians 3:3). Choosing to live a life under God's protection is not just a shield against day-to-day difficulties; it is an agreement to trade our best efforts at self-preservation for His.

1. Does the psalm assure the reader one will not suffer sickness or misfortune—or will even suffer less than an unbeliever? If not, what assurance does it offer? _____
   _____
   _____
   _____
   _____
   _____

2. Do we have any responsibility to avoid danger, given God's assurances of protection? Explain, citing Scripture if possible. _____
   _____
   _____
   _____
   _____

> ### Figure of Speech
>
> #### God's Wings
>
> The picture of a chicken or duck sheltering its young from the rain and cold by covering them with its wings is familiar to all of us. It is the very picture of nurturing and supportive love. It is as though the bird is shutting out the dangers and terrors of the world, comforting its young with the warmth of home.
>
> We should not assume God has wings like a bird. As with the rest of the figures in the psalm, the point is not to give a literal depiction of truth but rather an overall image. Our God is a constant source of encouragement, protection and hope to all those who take refuge in Him. As a young child instinctively retreats into the arms of a mother or father, so also God's children run to Him when fears abound.
>
> Tragically, this is not always the case. Jesus wept over Jerusalem in Matthew 23:37-39 because its inhabitants had rejected the love He had offered them. Ultimately, although God wants nothing more than to bring us into a close fellowship with Him, we must consciously make the decision to do so.

3. What are angels and what role (if any) do they serve for us? Cite Scripture. __
_____
_____
_____

4. What is your favorite line in the psalm and why? _____
_____
_____
_____

Life: A Bible Study

The nation of Israel, by any reasonable judgment, was dead. More than half of the nation had long since been scattered throughout the Assyrian empire for their rebellion—ten tribes, gone forever. The remaining "faithful" ones that remained were little better. In the days following the reign of the godly boy king Josiah, the people grew more and more ungodly, the leaders less and less interested in the word of God as presented by Jeremiah and other godly prophets. As Ezekiel ministered to the exiles in Babylonia, vainly trying to help them appreciate the depth of their rebellion, it was becoming more and more apparent the spiritual state of Judah had more than justified God's actions in taking away His people's land, freedom, and even the temple.

"Dead" is a relative term when it concerns God. Hebrews 11:17-19 tells us Abraham believed God was capable of raising Isaac from the dead if it was necessary for Him to keep His promises. Every once in awhile, God left reminders for the faithful that He could conquer any enemy that might come—even death itself.

When Ezekiel saw a vision of dried-out bones filling a valley (Ezekiel 37:1-14), bones as far removed from life and useful activity as could be, he likely had no difficulty seeing the connection God was making between them and His people. They had long since passed the point where they could offer Him anything He was willing to accept. To a holy man such as Ezekiel, a return from such a state must have seemed impossible.

But God gave them flesh. And then God gave them breath. Bones became fully human, fully alive, once again. Naturally, He did not mean that He would restore physical life to those who had passed away. He would give life to the nation itself. As He says in Ezekiel 37:14, "I will put My Spirit in you, and you will live, and I will settle you in your land. Then you will know that I am the LORD. I have spoken, and I will do it."

The dead, like Judah of old, may have little hope of resurrection; but, as with Judah, it is because they are trusting in themselves instead of "God who raises the dead" (2 Corinthians 1:9). And if we have hope He can raise us spiritually, we also have hope He will raise us physically on the last day (1 Corinthians 15:22). Just as life without God is not living, so also death with God is not dying.

Read Psalm 91 again—this time with Ezekiel in mind.

1. How might God's people lose spiritual vitality today? How can that process be reversed? _____
_____
_____
_____

2. Does shrinking attendance in a local church indicate the church is dying? Why or why not? _____
_____
_____
_____

Psalm 139—A Parallel Study

Parents know their children. They have watched them from the very beginning. They have observed their strengths and weaknesses, their successes and failures. They are aware of their physical defects, their character flaws, their personality quirks. After all, they have had virtually unfettered access. They could not be more emotionally engaged. Why would they be uninformed—especially concerning the important issues of life? From the other perspective, children can have confidence their parents are always present—in spirit if not in actual body. Although that may be an intimidating or unwelcome thing in particular situations, no child who enjoys a healthy relationship with his or her parents would want to escape from them. Whether the child picks up the phone or not, it is a blessing to know the line is open.

Such is the case even more so for God and His spiritual children. He is with us always. He provides assurance, guidance, discipline, hope, or whatever else might be needed at the time. He knows us intimately—everything we need, everything we do, everything we are. We can never escape His sight—and, if we have the relationship with Him we should, that's a splendid thing.

1. Verses 13-16 are often used to attach personhood to a human being even prior to birth. List some other passages that can be read in the same way. _____
   _____
   _____
   _____

2. Verse 17 tells us God's thoughts are difficult to comprehend. Explain the phrase. Does this mean the Bible is too tough for us to understand properly?
   _____
   _____
   _____

3. Why would God's child want Him to search his heart for "any offensive way" (v.24)? Should it not be a humiliation to be found lacking by our Father? ____
   _____
   _____
   _____

4. What is your favorite line in the psalm and why? _____
   _____
   _____
   _____

Life: A Case Study

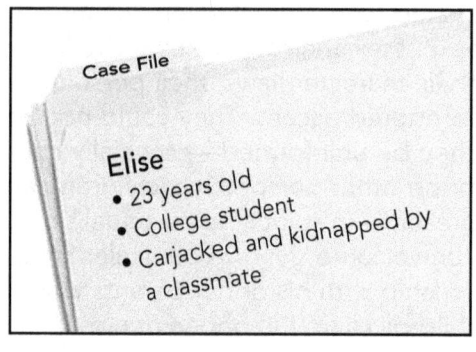

Everyone had heard. Naturally, everyone wanted to talk to her about it at church. A few brethren were hesitant to bring it up, thinking Elise might have considered it to be personal. But when it became obvious she didn't mind, she quickly became surrounded by sympathizers, well-wishers, admirers, and garden-variety thrill junkies. At one point, as the crowd kept growing and she found herself repeating herself, she raised her hands and said, "OK, I'm going to go through this one more time. After this, anyone who wants to know the story is going to have to talk to one of you.

"There's this guy in my economics class. He's in my study group. I always thought he was nice. Maybe a little creepy, not my type at all, but nice. Anyway, I was sitting in the coffee shop on campus studying when he just happened to come in and see me. That's what he said, anyway. Looking back now…anyway, we talked for a bit, and then he walked me out to my car. But when I got my keys out, he grabbed them out of my hand. He said, 'Why don't you let me drive?' By this point, I was getting a bit unnerved, but he was a lot bigger than me, so I decided just to go along with it.

"When we got in the car, he locked the doors and then pulled out a knife and stuck it in my ribs. He said, 'I don't want to hurt you; I just want to talk.' Well, my dad told me about boys who needed lethal weapons to 'talk' to girls. I had a pretty good idea where this was going.

"Suddenly I had a flash from Sunday morning's Bible study in Nehemiah—the part where Nehemiah says a quick prayer before making his request known to the king. I don't remember exactly how I phrased it. 'Help me, Lord,' 'Please get me out of this, Lord,' something like that. I didn't know quite what to do, but I knew, somehow, there was going to be a way out.

"That's when I noticed my Bible on the front dashboard. And I never keep it there. For whatever reason, I had left it in the car the night before. So I reached up and picked it up.

"Didn't he try to stop you?" someone asked.

"He did. He stuck the knife in my ribs—actually drew a little blood, I found out later. I just said, 'It's just my Bible. You're not really going to stab me because I'm reading my Bible, are you?' And I opened it up—to Psalm 91, as it turned out—and started reading out loud. He told me to stop at first, but I kept going.

It's insane to think about now—him driving my car 45 miles per hour down the road toward who knows where, me reading to him about God shielding His people and protecting them from harm.

"Anyway, just before I got to the end of the psalm, he just pulled over and got out of the car, leaving me and the keys behind. Didn't say a word."

"Did you call the police?"

"No, I just let him go. No real harm was done, other than maybe scaring me out of a few days of life. I'm sure he won't try it again."

"Do you think he'll be in class on Monday?"

Elise smiled. "I don't know. But I'm taking my Bible with me, just in case."

Read Psalm 91 again—this time with Elise in mind.

What would you say to Elise based on Psalm 91? _____
_____
_____
_____

New Testament Insight

For He will give His angels orders concerning you
to protect you in all your ways.   *— Psalm 91:11*

It doesn't take a Christian to know the Bible, or even to quote it. If an enemy of God and His people are using the Bible to further his cause, you can have some measure of confidence they are using it incorrectly.

Satan's quotation in Matthew 4:6 is an excellent example. To get Jesus to exert His will instead of pursuing His Father's will, he suggested Jesus throw himself from the pinnacle of the temple. After all, surely God would not allow His Son to die in such a manner, not after centuries of preparation for this time. But Jesus understood the nature of figurative language. He knew, although all Scripture is true, not all Scripture is given in literal language. The Psalms (as well as our ordinary speech) are filled with figures of speech. One who is inclined to understand them properly can do so with ease.

Additionally, Jesus understood the concept of the unity of Scripture. As God by one Spirit gave the word to us, it is inconceivable that one part of it should be working against another. And since one of the core tenets of Scripture is that we submit to God and not "test the Lord your God." As Jesus said (referencing Deuteronomy 6:16), He knew Psalm 91 could not possibly be saying we can place

In Heavenly Love Abiding

In heav'n-ly love a-bid-ing, No change my heart shall fear.
Wher-ev-er He may guide me, No want shall turn me back.
Green pas-tures are be-fore me, Which yet I have not seen.

And safe in such con-fid-ing, For noth-ing chang-es here.
My Shep-herd is be-side me, And noth-ing can I lack.
Bright skies will soon be o'er me, Where dark-est clouds have been.

The storm may roar with-out me, My heart may low be laid,
His wis-dom ev-er wak-eth; His sight is nev-er dim;
My hope I can-not mea-sure; My path to life is free.

But God is round a-bout me, And can I be dis-mayed?
He knows the way He tak-eth, And I will walk with Him.
My Sav-ior has my treas-ure, And He will walk with me.

1. And can— I be dis-mayed?

Words: Anna L. Waring
Music: Felix Mendelssohn, Op. 59

E♭ - 4 - SOL

ourselves in harm's way with confidence God will immediately and automatically come to our rescue.

Life: A Hymn Study

Anna Laetitia Waring was only 27 when she wrote: "In Heavenly Love Abiding." Born in 1823 in the Welsh town of Neath to Quaker parents, she became an avid Bible student early. She learned Hebrew in her youth so she could study the Old Testament in the original language. She acquired her talent for writing early as well, as her father and uncle were both writers. But she had an independent streak as well, which she showed as an adult in leaving her family heritage and being baptized into the Anglican church.

She self-published 39 hymns in two volumes of her poetry in the 1850s, the first of which included "In Heavenly Love Abiding." F.D. Huntington is credited with bringing her hymns to America in 1863.

"In Heavenly Love Abiding" has been paired with a half-dozen or more tunes over the last century and a half. The one most familiar to Christians is almost certainly the one derived from Felix Mendelssohn's Opus 59. The opus is a collection of six songs, intended to be sung a capella. "In Heavenly Love Abiding" borrows from the third of the six, "Abschied vom Walde" (which translates, "Farewell to the Forest").

Born Jakob Ludwig Felix Mendelssohn Bartholdy on February 3, 1809, Mendelssohn was baptized a Lutheran after being raised without religion by his Jewish parents. His music is particularly suited to adaptation for hymns and has often been used, perhaps most notably for Charles Wesley's "Hark, the Herald Angels Sing."

Life: A Worship Study

"I like that one a lot," said Enoch, one of the little ones who liked to sit in during our class. What he lacked in tunefulness he more than made up for in enthusiasm.

"I do too," I said. "'In Heavenly Love Abiding' has been one of my mother's favorite songs for as long as I can remember."

"Mine, too."

"Enoch, you have never sung that song in your life before," said her mother, Ellen.

"But it will be as long as I will remember," Enoch replied insistently. The logic in the mind of a 6-year-old has always intrigued me.

"I like it, too," said Enoch's teenage sister, Etta. "But I had a question about how 'The storm may roar without me.' Does that mean trouble is going to come if I'm not there, living as a Christian should?"

"I think 'without' is an old-fashioned way of saying 'outside,' I replied "as in, the opposite of 'within.' You're right about storms being symbolic of hardships. Lots of our hymns use that imagery. I think the point in this one is that life will constantly be filled with difficulties and setbacks, like walking through a constant thunderstorm. I mean, you're in eighth grade, right? You know all about that." Etta nodded vigorously.

"But no matter how tough life gets, we can make it. Because it's not just the storm that is out there. 'But God is round about me,' the next line reads. I think Miss Waring meant it's impossible to get too discouraged when God is with you every hour of every day."

"Do you think Miss Waring had a younger brother?" Etta asked. Enoch was busy racing around the room with a wastebasket over his head, claiming to be a killer robot from outer space.

I chuckled. "I don't know about that. But I suspect that God can give you peace when dealing with your younger brother if that is why you ask. What do you think?"

"I suppose so," said Etta, with an exaggerated sigh.

What does "In Heavenly Love Abiding" mean to you? _____
_____
_____
_____

The Bible Study Song List

If you were putting a list together for a study about life, what songs would you include and why? _____
_____
_____

What songs might you exclude and why? _____
_____
_____

www.ingramcontent.com/pod-product-compliance
Lightning Source LLC
LaVergne TN
LVHW061332060426
835512LV00013B/2613